H. Wiley Hitchcock, editor

Prentice-Hall
History of Music Series

MUSIC IN THE MEDIEVAL WORLD, *Albert Seay*

RENAISSANCE MUSIC, *Joel Newman*

BAROQUE MUSIC, *Claude V. Palisca*

MUSIC IN THE CLASSIC PERIOD, *Reinhard G. Pauly*

NINETEENTH-CENTURY ROMANTICISM IN MUSIC, *Rey M. Longyear*

TWENTIETH-CENTURY MUSIC: AN INTRODUCTION, *Eric Salzman*

FOLK AND TRADITIONAL MUSIC OF THE WESTERN CONTINENTS, *Bruno Nettl*

MUSIC CULTURES OF THE PACIFIC, THE NEAR EAST, AND ASIA, *William P. Malm*

MUSIC OF LATIN AMERICA, *Gilbert Chase*

MUSIC IN THE UNITED STATES: A HISTORICAL INTRODUCTION, *H. Wiley Hitchcock*

TWO HUNDRED YEARS OF RUSSIAN MUSIC, 1770-1970, *Boris Schwarz*

Twentieth-Century Music: An Introduction

ERIC SALZMAN
Composer

PRENTICE-HALL, INC., ENGLEWOOD CLIFFS, NEW JERSEY

for Lorna

Current printing (last digit):
10 9 8 7 6 5

Library of Congress Catalog Card Number: 67-22097

Printed in the United States of America

PRENTICE-HALL INTERNATIONAL, INC., *London*
PRENTICE-HALL OF AUSTRALIA, PTY. LTD., *Sydney*
PRENTICE-HALL OF CANADA, LTD., *Toronto*
PRENTICE-HALL OF INDIA (PRIVATE) LTD., *New Delhi*
PRENTICE-HALL OF JAPAN, INC., *Tokyo*

Foreword

Students and informed amateurs of the history of music have long needed a series of books that are comprehensive, authoritative, and engagingly written. They have needed books written by specialists—but specialists interested in communicating vividly. The Prentice-Hall History of Music Series aims at filling these needs.

Six books in the series present a panoramic view of the history of Western music, divided among the major historical periods—Medieval, Renaissance, Baroque, Classic, Romantic, and Contemporary. The musical cultures of the United States, Latin America, and Russia, viewed historically as independent developments within the larger western tradition, are discussed in three other books. In yet another pair, the rich yet neglected folk and traditional music of both hemispheres is treated. Taken together, the eleven volumes of the series are a

Foreword continued

distinctive and, we hope, distinguished contribution to the history of the music of the world's peoples. Each volume, moreover, may be read singly as a substantial account of the music of its period or area.

The authors of the series are scholars of national and international repute—musicologists, critics, and teachers of acknowledged stature in their respective fields of specialization. In their contributions to the Prentice-Hall History of Music Series their goal has been to present works of solid scholarship that are eminently readable, with significant insights into music as a part of the general intellectual and cultural life of man.

H. WILEY HITCHCOCK, *Editor*

Preface

In any consideration of the music of the twentieth century, it is necessary to begin by remembering that a good deal of it has not yet been written. Fortunately, twentieth-century music can reasonably be said to have begun somewhere about 1900; it is one of the few clear-cut chronological realities with which we can deal.

The history of culture can be thought of in many ways: as a succession of events (the way we tend, perhaps, to think about ancient history), as the movement of great historical forces (the way we think about the Renaissance and Reformation), in terms of social, political, and economic realities (our view of the Middle Ages and of the Baroque and Rococo-Classical periods as well) or in terms of creative personalities (the Romantic view). As this series of books itself can testify, these conceptions need not be mutually exclusive and none of them need preclude an understanding of cultural history as a history of ideas. Without, I hope, entirely forgetting any of the former, it is the last-named that I have tried to write: the creative development of musical ideas in the last sixty-five years understood against and as distinct from the past, in the variety and unity of its own internal growth and in its potential for the future.

It is my hope and belief that a book of this kind, which deals primarily and directly with musical ideas and materials, can bring the reader towards the musical experience itself, in terms of the greatest variety and richness of ideas and expression, a richness itself characteristic of the twentieth-century musical experience. Towards this end, certain sacrifices have consciously been made. Detailed biographical information will have to be sought elsewhere (such things are, except in the cases of the very youngest composers, available in standard reference works). Analytic material has been limited to a few indicative examples—it is always to be assumed that, on every page of this book, the reader is being actually referred to the music itself. No attempt has been made to achieve the illusory goal of completeness and long lists of also-rans have been avoided. I am well aware that Florent Schmitt, Franz Schreker, Ghedini, Grainger and Glière, Weiner and Weinberger, Alfven, Zemlinsky, and a host of greater and lesser lights do not appear and that others, particularly—but not exclusively—composers of more national or local significance, receive only brief consideration. I am also conscious of the fact that the work of certain composers—particularly since World War II—inevitably receives a certain emphasis because it lends itself easily to verbal analysis or description, qualities which do not necessarily correspond to artistic values. The deficiencies of this book with respect to American music are, fortunately, compensated for by the inclusion in this series of a volume by H. Wiley Hitchcock devoted entirely to the subject. It is the intention here to treat the development of American music in our century in terms of the general development of twentieth-century ideas everywhere; it is, surprisingly enough (and limited as it is), one of the first such attempts. In any case, I can only hope that, in a book intended to be devoted to essentials, the essentials are there.

There are other problems to which attention should be called, particularly those which derive from the closeness, contemporaneity, and changeability of the subject matter. I would like to make a special mention of one of these. Even in a book which deals, first of all, with creative ideas rather than documentation, the question of chronology is important. It is the past which is studied by historians; the musicology of modern times is necessarily incomplete. The dates which appear in the standard reference works, in printed chronologies, in the studies which have so far appeared, in program notes or even on the scores themselves may (when accurate) represent the date of completion, of copyright, of publication, or even of first performance. Whenever possible, I have attempted to give what are, according to my best knowledge and information, the actual years of composition. I can only add that I believe that the errors or imprecisions of date which will have crept into the book do not affect any of its premises.

Among many debts, I wish to acknowledge here at least these few: to H. Wiley Hitchcock in his triple role as chairman of the music department at Hunter College (in which capacity he invited me to give the course out of which many of the ideas of this book have come), as the understanding and skillful editor of this series, and as the author of the volume on American music without which any understanding of the material in this book is necessarily incomplete; to my teachers Roger Sessions and Milton Babbitt for their profound insight into the nature and meaning of the musical process; to Ross Parmenter, former Music Editor of *The New York Times*, who was responsible, both as editor and as a remarkable kind of mentor, for the beginning of my career as a critic; to the Ford Foundation for having enabled me to renew first-hand my acquaintance with European musical life; and, finally, to that extraordinary young generation of performing musicians who have made possible a vital, new, contemporary musical life.

E. S.

Contents

I

Twentieth-Century Music and the Past

The music of the twentieth century seems so fundamentally different from the music of the past and so varied and wide-ranging in itself that it is difficult to realize that the music of our time has deep roots in what came before and, at the same time, a pervasive unity that distinguishes it from its past.

The history of creativity in Western music since 1900 is inconceivable without the history of Western music in the preceding centuries; our musical institutions and, indeed, our whole way of thinking about music are inheritances from the recent and not-so-recent past, and in certain fundamental ways the tradition has continued to exert its influence even on the greatest innovators.[1] Nevertheless we can also attempt to define a distinctly twentieth-century viewpoint when we recognize that nearly all the creative musical thinking of our century—even that which is described as "conservative"—has participated in the search for new forms. The old forms, the old expressive structures, can be comprehended by the term "functional tonality" understood in its broadest traditional sense, embracing ideas and "expression" on the one hand and underlying structural, organizing principles on the other. After 1900 the old propositions ceased to function as *a priori* assumptions; related to the tradition or not, tonal or non–tonal, conservative or revolutionary, all twentieth-century musical art has had to establish its own expressive and intellectual premises.

In spite of technological, social, and esthetic upheaval, contemporary musical ideas are still communicated in the context of musical life whose structure, means, and institutions are largely derived from the late eighteenth and nineteenth centuries.[2] This is true of our concert and operatic institutions, of our instruments (even the old violins have been so largely rebuilt that they can be considered nineteenth-century instruments), and of instrumental technique. It is true of the modern orchestra, of our chamber music ensembles, of our operatic forms, of the virtuoso soloist, and of the solo recital. Similarly, the bulk of our musical repertory, our techniques of teaching the practice and theory of music (and the institution of the conservatory itself), as well as most of our artistic and esthetic notions and assumptions about what music is and what it ought to do—all these things reached their full development between 1700 and 1900 and have been bequeathed to us surprisingly intact.

Some of our most fundamental ways of thinking about music and musical creation are also inheritances from the recent past. Indeed, our whole notion of "art" and artistic creation as a unique and separable human activity is a relatively modern Western idea, by no means universal in human experience, and one which strongly links the "romantic" era with the twentieth century. The notion of the creation and experience of music for its own sake is one that entered Western musical culture at a recent date, and in spite of many attempts in the last decades to modify this rather special conception of the role of music in our society, we still tend to think of the highest forms of music making as the purest—that is, the most isolated and detached from other forms of human activity. Like

[1] When historians talk about "modern" European history, they mean "since the French Revolution." Similarly, "modern art" surveys begin with David and Goya. Only in music is there general agreement not to treat this time span as one period.

[2] This is not a book that deals with the development of musical ideas in relationship to general history. Clearly, however, two world wars and the social, political, technological, and scientific revolutions of the twentieth century have had a meaning for contemporary culture parallel to the impact that the fall of the *ancien régime*, Napoleon, the Industrial Revolution, and the new bourgeois society had on the life and thought of the nineteenth.

our nineteenth-century forebears, we think of the composer as a creative individual communicating personal, original, and unique thoughts with a distinctive style and a particularized point of view and expression. This concept of the composer—derived from the romantic idea of the artist as a culture hero—has led us to place greater emphasis than ever on creative individuality, originality, and freedom. Finally, the nineteenth century taught us to understand the work of art as conditioned by its historical and cultural context and, at the same time and without contradiction, as an individual expression of artistic uniqueness. The very notion of "the avant-garde" as it is usually understood is a nineteenth-century, romantic conception.

We can expect then to comprehend a great deal of what has happened in the twentieth century in terms of the past. Just as the historical personalities of Beethoven and Wagner remain decisive in the formation of our conceptions of the role of the composer in society, so does the music of Beethoven and Wagner suggest the development of ideas and techniques which evolved into characteristic twentieth-century modes of musical thought. The modulatory freedom in Beethoven's music stands in a direct relationship to the chromatic freedom and incipient "atonality" of *Tristan und Isolde* and, in turn, Wagner's expanded palette of orchestral, harmonic, and contrapuntal techniques can be clearly traced in the music of composers like Richard Strauss, Gustav Mahler, and even César Franck and Gabriel Fauré. The revival and refinement of classical organizational principles and the close relation of these to modern structural ideas of a music that is totally organic and interrelated is already basic in the music of Brahms. The resources of harmonic and melodic patterns that lie outside of the major-minor functional tonality system are suggested by the music of composers like Mussorgsky and even Dvořák. The "back-to-Bach" movement and the rediscovery of "pre-Bach" music and musical forms were accomplished facts long before 1900. In short, chromaticism; the extended and freer use of dissonance; the establishment of harmonic and melodic freedom; the use of harmonic, melodic, and structural ideas derived from folk music and early Western music; the concept of the structural interrelationships between all the parts of a musical composition; the discovery of the distant past and of non-Western music; the vast expansion of instrumental technique and color; the new freedom, complexity, and independence of rhythm, dynamics, and tone color—all these modern ideas have roots deep in the last century.

Less obvious, perhaps, but equally important is the persistence of certain underlying modes of musical thought, especially those dealing with large statement and structure—complex and subtle ideas built up over the course of many generations and not easily dissipated even by revolutionary changes on the surface. There is a central development of musical thinking that connects Haydn directly with Mahler in a line of structural conceptions that constantly increase in size and scope. This kind of thinking remains surprisingly operative in the twentieth century—in the many attempts to revive and renew "sonata form," for example, or in a more profound way, in the development of chromatic and twelve-tone structures in the work of the Viennese, the direct inheritors of the "main line" tradition.

More than anything else, however, the romantic notion of the artist as an individualist has helped to form the modern impulse towards originality and uniqueness. In a sense, the vast and swift changes in all modern art can be seen as an intensification of a historical process of change that has long been operative in Western culture. But even if we accept the premise that the vast expansion of vocabulary and means in this century is part of an over-all process taking place over the past centuries, there is reason to believe that, after a point, the character of the process itself changes and quantitative distinctions become clearly qualitative. For our purposes, we can define that point as the moment when traditional tonality ceased to provide the fundamental expressive and organizational foundation of musical thought and was replaced by other modes of musical expression and organization. This change actually occurred in the years around 1900 and it is this fact that enables us to speak distinctively of the music of the twentieth century.

Western music between about 1600 and 1900 was distinguished by the developing and characteristic kind of musical thinking that we have termed "functional tonality." Traditionally, the word "tonality" is defined in a crude way as a representation of a basic scale formation within which certain hierarchies prevail—expressed as points of stability and instability. Even within this rough and simplistic definition we can grasp the notion that certain tones and combinations of tones represent goals and suggest stability and rest, while others imply motion to or away from these goals. Tonality, then, in its traditional form, presents a principle of order in musical thought which implies that every formation of horizontal and vertical (that is, melodic and harmonic) tones has a definable relationship to every other such formation. To express the idea in another way, every musical event has a "function" or a functional role which relates it to what has come before and what will happen next. The basic psychological principle here is expectation; the basic musical technique is that of direction and motion. Out of this grow the characteristic ways in which musical lines will rise and fall and the ways in which simultaneous musical lines will relate to one another in harmonic patterns. The idea of expectation suggests the use of resolution and non-resolution; of so-called dissonance and consonance; of intensity and relaxation; of cadence, accent, and articulation; of phrase and punctuation; of rhythm and dynamic; even of tempo and tone color.

Out of these apparently simple psychological and musical facts evolved one of the most complex and sophisticated modes of artistic expression that man has ever developed. The concept of primary goals suggested the possibility of secondary goals, the idea of "modulation," in which musical motion could turn away from its primary centers of gravity to secondary centers which could then serve to reinforce the motion back to the primary ones. This made possible the complex structures of eighteenth- and nineteenth-century music, with their web of relationships which, unfolding in time, tie every note of a piece firmly to every other note. When we say that Beethoven's "Eroica" Symphony is in E–flat, we are saying much more than the fact that its first and last harmonies are E–flat major triads; we are implying a whole way of thinking about the organization of sound which determines every aspect of our experience of the music.[3]

Characteristic forms of tonal expression, contrast, interrelationship, and structure guided musical thinking for three centuries. Except to a limited degree in certain forms of folk and popular music, they are no longer operative; since the opening years of this century, composers have ceased to accept the unquestioned validity of these concepts. Wagner's extreme chromatic freedom, "atonal" as it may seem at times, is still based on the listener's expectation that one musical event implies another— *Tristan* is built on the very idea of the defeat of expectation. The music of Debussy, Schoenberg, and Stravinsky, however, no longer depends on that expectation but sets forth new kinds of definitions and relationships. Even the most conservative twentieth-century music establishes forms of motion and rest with new means. When Beethoven uses the familiar dominant-tonic cadence, it has a formal and expressive significance that is inseparable from the entire fabric and structure of the musical thought; when the same musical event occurs in Prokofiev, it is a local incident whose significance must be understood in other terms. It is true that certain underlying universal principles have retained force and validity, but since 1900 there has no longer been any necessary and prior assumption—any generally accepted premise preceding the fact of musical composition—that would strictly imply that any one musical realization must follow or be derived from any other.

The development of creative musical thought since 1900 has been rich and complex, full of remarkable achievements, remarkable and unremarkable failures, enormous and continuing promise, and seemingly endless contradiction. There is some reason to believe that the developments of the last few years, particularly with respect to electronic means (mostly utilized until now for the reproduction of traditional ideas) and new instrumental and vocal techniques and ideas, mark a more definitive break with the past—for better or for worse—than anything accomplished up until now. But all twentieth-century music can be understood as a unity if it is understood against the background of the past and the dominating tonal ideas of that past. Once this unity, essentially negative in its nature,

---

[3] The vexed question of "classical" tonality is obviously not so simple; the foregoing is intended to be suggestive rather than definitive. Most modern views about the encompassing function of the old tonality derive from the writings of the German theorist Heinrich Schenker.

has been grasped, we can begin to understand the positive ways in which contemporary creative thought has redefined its intellectual, expressive, and creative aims. The history of music in the twentieth century can be understood in terms of two great cycles: first, the abandonment of functional tonality after 1900, the explorations of vast new materials before and after World War I, and the new tonal and twelve-tone syntheses that followed; and second, the very different but parallel set of rejections, new beginnings, explorations, analyses, and syntheses following World War II. The bond that connects all of twentieth-century music grows out of the fact that each composer—and each piece—has had to establish new and unique forms of expressive and intellectual communication. To understand the music of this century, we must examine these forms.

Bibliography

The general literature in English on the music and musical ideas of the twentieth century is neither large nor distinguished. The pioneer efforts of Marion Bauer (*Twentieth Century Music*, New York, 1933, rev. 1947) and Aaron Copland (*Our New Music*, New York, 1941) are no longer serviceable, and the books of Adolfo Salazar (*Music in Our Time*, New York, 1946), Paul Collaer (*A History of Modern Music*, Cleveland, 1961, paperback, New York, 1963) and André Hodeir (*Since Debussy*, New York, 1961) are imbalanced and/or poorly translated. There are two books on *European Music in the Twentieth Century* (ed. Howard Hartog, New York and London, 1957; Arthur Cohn, New York, 1965), one on *Contemporary Music in Europe* (New York, 1963) and two called *This Modern Music* (John Tasker Howard, New York, 1942; Gerald Abraham, New York, 1952). Of the several books published in London in recent years, two collections of essays may be mentioned: Wilfred Mellers' *Studies in Contemporary Music* (1947; largely devoted to lesser figures) and Donald Mitchell's *The Language of Modern Music* (1963; concerned with major personalities and major premises). The short book by Peter Hansen (*An Introduction to Twentieth-Century Music*, Boston, 1961) and Joseph Machlis' *Introduction to Contemporary Music* (New York, 1961) virtually complete the list of surveys in English.

Special mention should be made of Nicolas Slonimsky's astonishing year-by-year documentary *Music Since 1900* (3rd ed., New York, 1949). There are a number of "popular" and "appreciation" books, but the standard music dictionaries are better (though not ideal) sources of information in English.

Several attempts have been made to produce generalized studies of twentieth-century materials and methods intended as theoretical statements or teaching matter; only one or two of these, connected with the work of particular composers, will concern us (see the relevant chapters of this book). The reader's attention, however, is called to the following specialized periodicals: *Perspectives of New Music* (Princeton); *Journal of Music Theory* (New Haven); *The Score* (London); *Die Reihe* (Vienna; Eng. tr., Bryn Mawr, Pa.); *Melos* and *Darmstädter Beiträge zur Neuen Musik* (both Mainz, Germany). [William Austin's substantial *Music in the 20th Century* (New York, 1966) was published after the foregoing was written. *Ed.*]

PART TWO

The
Breakdown
of
Traditional
Tonality

2

The Sources

A major contribution to the development of the large tonal structures of the eighteenth and nineteenth centuries was the expansion of the use and meaning of chromatic inflection. A basic characteristic of traditional tonality in its fully developed form was the structural use of modulation, out of which grew the large symphonic forms which are its great intellectual achievement. Yet, in the evolution of things, it was modulation and its local allies, secondary dominants and altered chords, that were ultimately to undermine that tonality. Chromaticism pre-dates classical tonality, of course, but it came to play a particular structural role— through the technique of modulation—in the growth of tonal forms in the seventeenth century. Through the eighteenth and nineteenth centuries, it played an increasingly important role in the creation of large tonal structures by delaying and ultimately reinforcing the musical motion of a piece towards its tonic. In the classical and romantic symphony, modulation and chromaticism were essential in the formation of large structures. With many of the romantic composers, Chopin and Liszt for example, chromaticism played its major role in matters of expressive detail; in Brahms and, especially, in the gigantic structures of the Wagnerian music drama, it functioned both as detail and as the basis for structural prolongation. *Tristan und Isolde* is still part of the tradition in that its extreme chromaticism is still based on expectation defeated by "false" and evasive resolution, harmonic delay, and long-range suspension. Nevertheless, in parts of *Tristan* and *Parsifal* we are at the point where a quantitative development is very nearly a qualitative one.

Tristan und Isolde was first performed in 1865, but, in a way, its influence did not become decisive until the end of the century. None of the direct heirs of the Wagner tradition—Bruckner, Strauss, even Mahler —was primarily concerned with the development of Tristanesque chromatic procedures, although each of them employed the new harmonic, melodic, and modulatory freedom as the basis for a late–romantic, tonal style. The only post-Wagnerian who used a complex chromatic idiom was Max Reger (1873–1916), but Reger's chromaticism is carefully systematized and based on eighteenth-century forms and procedures derived from Bach and Mozart. Reger had a certain influence—mainly theoretical—on Hindemith; otherwise his significance for the twentieth century is small.

The composer who most directly and completely connects late Wagner and the twentieth century is Arnold Schoenberg (1874–1951). The inventor of twelve-tone music began his career in perfect Tristanesque Wagnerianism, and in works like *Verklärte Nacht* (1899), the *Gurrelieder* cycle (1901; orchestrated 1910), *Pelleas und Melisande* (1902–1903), and the First and Second String Quartets (1905, 1907) the implications of *Tristan* and *Parsifal* are carried forward, eventually beyond the realm of tonal expectation and tonal form. By contrast, Richard Strauss (1864–1949) and Gustav Mahler (1860–1911) absorbed *Tristan* into their composing equipment along with the entire Wagnerian arsenal of new techniques. Strauss developed few new techniques and, essentially, he found no new universal forms. His style up to and perhaps including *Der Rosenkavalier* (1909–1910) suggests not so much a development from as a thorough exploration of the implications of the Wagnerian revolution. But it is as impossible to deny the impact of works like *Salome* (1903–1905) and *Elektra* (1906–1908) on the early development of twentieth-century music as it is difficult today to appreciate and assess the significance of that impact. Perhaps the relationship is clearest on the dramatic-psychological plane; we would call it Freudian and trace its influence on the development of "expressionist" musical theatre in works like Schoenberg's *Erwartung* and Berg's *Wozzeck* and *Lulu*. Musically, we can see two important contributions. In the small, Strauss finds it possible—in a way that Wagner never did—to delay or even omit the resolution of harmonic and melodic "dissonance"; in the large, he extends this principle of free, "dissonant" motion to produce "free association" forms which often defeat the natural and expected phrase-motion with breaks in the continuity of thought and with abrupt confrontations and juxtapositions which obviously derive from dramatic-psychological considerations. However, Strauss never really abandons functional tonality; it is somehow still operative, and, at the very moment when he seemed to be on the point of destroying it, he turned—first in *Der Rosenkavalier* and then definitively in *Ariadne auf Naxos* (1911–1912)—to classical forms and techniques in a clear attempt to reinstate it. *Ariadne* is, in effect, the first piece of neo-classicism; it pre-dates Stravinskyian neo-classicism by a number of years. But, as we shall see, Stravinsky's neo-tonality is synthetic; Stravinsky actually had to go through the process of destroying functional tonality and then inventing a new kind of tonality to replace it. Strauss never went that far; he went to the edge of the abyss and then turned back. He redefined his own limits as those of functional tonality. Strauss lived through nearly half of the twentieth century, long enough to become the only significant composer who still fully accepted and believed in those limitations.[1]

The case of Mahler is still more complex. To some extent, he can be said to have duplicated the Wagnerian revolution in symphonic music, partly by adapting the symphonic tradition to a vocal and lyric-dramatic conception of musical discourse (achieved, to a great extent, through the intermediate forms and techniques of the late-romantic lied as represented, for example, in the work of a composer like Hugo Wolf). Mahler's basic language is the common practice of the nineteenth century—securely tonal, even fundamentally diatonic. Through the long, long extension of lyric, melodic lines, an ever-extended delay of the cadence, a magnificent long-range harmonic motion, careful planning and pacing of dynamic and rhythmic curves, and extensive and skillful modulation, he extended relatively simple and apparently limited ideas into enormous and powerful structures. Mahler, in fact, built entire structures on a complex interrelationship of tonal areas to the point where, although detail is always clearly set forth in terms of tonal function, the long-range motion builds up in new tonal shapes; these large-scale compositions move successively through wider and wider ranges of tonal areas and often resolve themselves in tonal regions far from those in which they have set out. Thus, although Mahler seems in one sense to have escaped the tonal crises of the early years of the century, his essentially new view of tonal form as well as his remarkable

[1] Conscious "classicism" can be found in many Strauss works after *Der Rosenkavalier;* a good case can be made for a kind of new tonal resynthesis in some of the composer's late works, parallel in some important respects to Schoenberg's "non-tonal" synthesis; see, especially, the *Metamorphosen* for 23 solo strings of 1945.

Bust of Gustav Mahler by Rodin, which is on display in Philharmonic Hall, Lincoln Center for the Performing Arts. © 1965, Lincoln Center for the Performing Arts. Photographed by Bob Serating Photo, New York.

expansion of phrase-structure and of the use and organization of modulation and color has had an important influence in the twentieth century.[2]

One important late romantic remains to be mentioned here: the enigmatic Ferruccio Busoni (1866–1924). In his teaching and writing about music, notably in the *Sketch for a New Esthetic of Music* published in 1907, the famous piano virtuoso anticipated part of the development of contemporary ideas with visionary clarity. But his own vast output escapes the late nineteenth century only occasionally: in the use of chromatic, expressive dissonance in a few late works like the *Elegies* for piano of 1907 and in the intense contrapuntal chromaticism of some of the other keyboard works. Like Reger, Busoni's chromatic practice was as much a return to eighteenth-century ideals as a derivation from Wagner; however, the idea of a "neo-classical" chromaticism seems to have had —unless one excepts certain works of Schoenberg—no important development.

The tonal tradition in its most typical forms is Italo-German, and it can be said to have passed away in Central Europe by virtue of its own contrapuntal, chromatic development. Elsewhere this tonal tradition was much weaker, and once the overwhelming domination of Italian and German style had been shaken off, other, older traditions could rise to the surface and lead to new ideas. In Eastern Europe, for example, the romantic rediscovery of folk music had a decided impact on tonal ideas. While the folk music of Germany, Austria, and Italy[3] actually seems to have accommodated itself over the years to classical tonal organization, the traditional music of Hungary and the Slavic countries always maintained its modal independence, and even the so-called Hungarian-Gypsy music of Liszt and Brahms[4] suggests certain melodic usages (and a harmonic carry-over) at variance with common diatonic tonal usage. Eastern modal ideas show up in the work of composers like Dvořák and the Russian "Five" (although tonally accommodated); in the case of a Mussorgsky, such ideas were decisive in forming a melodic and harmonic style which often contradicted prevailing contrapuntal-tonal notions. (The performing editions of Rimsky-Korsakov and other well-wishers were designed to eliminate or smooth out such "crudities.")

One highly-developed Western art-music tradition has consistently remained somewhat outside the central development: that of France. Although the classical abstract formulation of tonal usage derives from the theoretical writings of Rameau, the actual evolution of French practice

[2] Mahler had, of course, a more direct and superficial influence, most notably on the modern Russian symphony.

[3] For pre-tonal forms in German folk music, see early chorale settings; in Italy, a pre-tonal folk music has persisted outside of the main urban centers.

[4] Both of these composers had, of course, a direct influence on posterity. Schoenberg has written eloquently of the intellectual impact of Brahms on modern musical thought; Liszt, who was an innovator in practically every musical domain, has been said to have prefigured nearly everyone from Wagner to Berg.

has taken place quite independently of the Italian-German tonal evolution. Characteristic of this independence is a metrical, rhythmic, and phrase flexibility closely related to the free non-accentual character of the French language. This relative freedom from "tonic" accent confers on French music a quality of fluid, poetical prose as opposed to the metrical "verse" construction of Italian and German music; in turn, French music often seems much less directional and much more coloristic. The independence was very persistent in the eighteenth century; it was less noticeable in the nineteenth, when French composers—Berlioz is a notable exception—tended to accept classical Italian and German rhythmic and structural forms. The influence of Wagner was as decisive in the latter part of the century as that of the classical masters had been earlier, but Wagner at least could suggest fluid prose and expressive color, and the French version of Wagnerian chromaticism is a very distinct if minor development with consequences for the twentieth century. One characteristic form of Wagnerian chromaticism came to France by way of Belgium through the work and influence of César Franck. Franck and the Franckophiles, Vincent D'Indy and Ernest Chausson (D'Indy's pupil, Albert Roussel, carried the line into still another generation), used extensive schemes of chromatic modulation combined with a flexible, asymmetrical sense of line and a tendency for rich, chromatic harmonies to shade off into color inflections in a very French way. Henri Duparc (a kind of French Hugo Wolf), Guillaume Lekeu (another Belgian) and Emmanuel Chabrier (at different times the most Wagnerian and the most anti-Wagnerian of French composers) all made their Bayreuth pilgrimages. Equally important, the literary influence of Wagner, particularly as transmitted through the work of the "symbolist" poets, played no small role in creating the rather special esthetic and intellectual atmosphere of *fin-de-siècle* Paris.

The tendency towards a flexible melodic style joined to a rich, sensuous, subtle harmonic palette is most highly developed (and most free of Wagnerianism) in the work of Gabriel Fauré (1845–1924), a composer who developed his poetic, evanescent chromaticism within the bounds of a complex, refined sense of tonal structure. Fauré, like Reger and Mahler, never left the confines of functional tonality, and his influence on later developments was only peripheral, but the freedom and subtlety of his style represent the artistic climate in France in the late nineteenth century and suggest, in a way parallel to Debussy, the coming tonal revolutions.

Bibliography

The sources of contemporary music—unlike the origins of modern art—have received little serious attention. One of the few important studies in this field, Ernst Kurth's *Romantische Harmonik und ihrer Krise in Wagners "Tris-*

tan" (Berlin, 1921), has never been translated into English. Elliott Zuckerman's *The First Hundred Years of Wagner's "Tristan"* (New York, 1964) is stronger on literary than musical matters. On the French background there is Martin Cooper's *French Music, from the Death of Berlioz to the Death of Fauré* (London, 1951). More specialized books include Dika Newlin's *Bruckner, Mahler, Schoenberg* (New York, 1947) and two multi-volume studies still in progress, Donald Mitchell's Mahler study (London, v. 1, 1958) and Norman del Mar's *Richard Strauss* (London, 1962). Romain Rolland's *Musicians of Today* (Paris, 1908; tr. New York, 1915) has the status of a document; so do the Busoni *Sketch* (Eng. tr. reprinted in *Three Classics in the Aesthetic of Music*, New York, 1962) and the various writings of Schoenberg (see *Harmonielehre*, Vienna, 1911; abridged tr. as *Theory of Harmony*, New York, 1948; see also essays in *Style and Idea*, New York, 1950).

3

The Revolution: Paris

In the late nineteenth century, Paris regained its old position as intellectual and artistic center of the West. Native musical tradition was not strong: the *Opéra* reigned supreme and the operatic tradition was that of Meyerbeer, Offenbach, and the Italians, tempered by the genteel sentimentalities of Gounod; there was a revival of symphonic and chamber music, but it was dominated by a watered-down classicism. The answer to this "philistinism" and "academicism" was Wagnerism; Wagner had had an overwhelming impact on French intellectual life not yet absorbed or overcome. But the Paris of the post-Prussian War period had an enormous intellectual and artistic vitality of its own, especially in the visual arts (academic and impressionist) and in literature; the line that descends from Baudelaire to Mallarmé and to the twentieth century also left deep traces on the history of music. *Fin-de-siècle* sensibility and a conscious search for new forms and new means combined with a rather special French refinement and subtle, abstracted sensuality. We recognize the kind of sensibility that we find in Mallarmé also in Fauré and, especially, in Debussy.

Erik Satie by Jean Cocteau. Meyer Collection, Paris. Reproduction forbidden.

There was another aspect to the intellectual style of the times: a mordant, dry, ironic wit. In the visual arts, it appears in the work of an artist like Toulouse-Lautrec; in music, it turns up in Chabrier as a conscious antidote to Wagnerism. But its most important musical exponent was Erik Satie (1866–1925), a remarkable innovator with a great deal of genius if little talent. Satie came to music late and never really mastered even his own ideas; his remarkable inventions were almost off-hand: casual, amusing discoveries which took form as literary wit. Satie constructed aphorisms and then turned them into simple musical expressions. As often as not, the point is in the idea, the title: "Cold Pieces," "Three Pieces in the Form of a Pear," "Truly Flabby Preludes," "Automatic Descriptions," "Disagreeable Impressions."

Satie was by no means the only example of a French composer at the turn of the century who tried to break with the past in an attempt to make music a vehicle for some kind of literary taste; the thing was in the air. And, ultimately, although Satie had both an immediate and a long-range influence, a great deal of his work was in fact produced in the shade of composers far more fitted than he to accomplish the break with traditional

Left to right: Stravinsky, Diaghilev, Cocteau, and Satie (dated 1917). Sketch by M. Larionov. Meyer Collection, Paris. Reproduction forbidden.

formal techniques that he so clearly foreshadowed. But he continues to occupy a special place in the history of recent music, not only as the godfather to a generation of composers but as a spiritual grandfather of latter-day avant-gardism. He was the first to *use* sound—disconnected, static, objectified sound—in an abstract way, essentially divorced from the organizational and structural principles of tonal form and development. The importance of this is as great as the actual results in Satie's music are trivial; except in the very smallest works, there is generally a large gap between the proposition of each piece—musical or literary—and the meaningful realization of its ideas.

Debussy

The problem of finding new modes of discourse, of replacing classical developmental-variational principles of tonality with new content and new expressive form, occupied the best musical minds in the decades around 1900. In Germany and Austria, the process had a strongly evolutionary aspect, growing out of the inner development of the tradition itself. In France, where classical tonality was much less firmly rooted or, in any event, more artificially cultivated, the break occurred earlier and with greater ease and thoroughness. We have discussed a number of people who helped to bring this about; but by far the most important was Claude Debussy. Debussy was, from the start, further removed from Bach and Beethoven than Schoenberg ever could be; *La Mer* has less to do with fugues and sonatas than even the most radical works of the Viennese.

Debussy (1862–1918), like most French composers, was intensively trained in the Central European classical tradition. The French Conservatoire, where he spent eleven years, has—since the reign of an Italian, Luigi Cherubini—always specialized in the very principles, techniques, and forms which have not been especially characteristic of French musical creativity.[1] To some extent, French music has been stifled by this, but for Debussy it was a source of strength. All the first great innovators of the twentieth century—Debussy, Stravinsky, the Viennese—met the challenge of the classical tradition and the classical disciplines in one way or another. But it is a curious fact that Debussy, in many ways the most independent of that tradition, was the only one to have had an intense classical conservatory training. For Schoenberg, the tradition provided an intellectual model and suggested underlying universal principles; for Debussy, it was a matter of métier, of fluency, and of complete, natural control.

Debussy's innovations, while expressed in great part in instrumental works, were based to some extent on the special and subtle inflections of

[1] This is not so surprising as it might seem. In the history of art, theory generally *follows* practice and codification is most easily performed, not by a practitioner, but by someone on the outside—in space or time—looking in.

French language and poetry; on the character and length of sound (as opposed to strong metrical and rhythmic accent); on the fluid and non-symmetrical organization of French meter, rhythm, accent, and phrase. Debussy extended this kind of rhythmical and phrase organization into every aspect of music: thus melodic, harmonic, rhythmic, and timbral ideas, blended and unified in essentially new ways, are organized around

Claude Debussy. Sketch by Henri Detouche. Meyer Collection, Paris. Reproduction forbidden.

qualities of sound patterns and relationships rather than around the significance of these in an overall rhythmic, phrase, and contrapuntal scheme. Melody, harmony, rhythm, and color become different aspects of a single basic conception; sounds and sound patterns are related to one other by arbitrary and sensual aural criteria rather than by the old necessities of motion and resolution governed by linear, tonal logic. Debussy was able —and this was his genius—to organize these new relationships into new forms which retain their psychological and even organic intellectual validity without depending on previously accepted conventions of tonal language and structure. In *Tristan*, even ultra-chromaticism and the most extended false resolutions are still governed by the laws of tonal motion and expectation; in *Pelléas et Mélisande* no such criteria are operative. Debussy's vocabulary of sound is chosen for its empirical (i.e., "sensual" in both meanings) qualities, and the motion from one sound pattern to the next is built on intervallic relationships and on parallelisms of structure, using very clear, immediate, and localized aural and psychological insights. In Debussy's earlier work, the simple and classical patterns of contrast and return still govern the large forms; later even these vanish, to be replaced by on-going associative forms which depart from one point and, even without the necessity of substantive recapitulation, arrive at another. In a sense, this non-narrative, non-cyclical form—achieved by Debussy in a work like the ballet *Jeux* of 1912—represents the larger intellectual tendency of the pre-World War I revolutions which we call "atonal." While our experience of complex chromatic forms over the last sixty or seventy years allows us to accept the new tonal relationships in Debussy as unexceptional and even traditional, there is no question that works like *La Mer* and *Jeux* mark as thorough and significant a break with the tonal tradition as any of the most complex works of Schoenberg or his colleagues.

Like many of his contemporaries, Debussy was influenced not only by the implications of the French language with all its freedom of flow and restricted yet fluid structure, but also by the prevailing literary culture of France. This esthetic, partly Wagnerian in origin, was allied with the late-romantic ideal of expressive musical poetry, and until his last few works, Debussy was generally concerned with expressive subjects, programs, and texts closely associated with the work of the "symbolist" poets: the *Prélude à l'après-midi d'un faune* of 1892–1894 (after Mallarmé), *La Mer* of 1902–1905, *Images* for orchestra of 1909, the various sets of piano pieces written between the 1880's and 1910, and, of course, the songs and theatrical works. It is a mistake to ignore the importance of non-musical, poetic ideas on the development of Debussy's musical ideas and the forms of his musical thought, but it is equally important to realize that his expressive and poetic intent can be understood in strictly musical terms as well.

It is often suggested that the whole-tone scale forms the basis of

Debussy's musical technique, with the implication that the old seven-note major-minor scale hierarchies have been replaced by the ambiguities of the six-note whole-step scale. However, in point of fact, whole-tone relationships are used by Debussy in conjunction with, or as part of, a much more complex group of melodic and harmonic usages—interlocking pentatonic forms, for example—based on the fundamental principle of symmetry. The whole-tone scale itself is, of course, symmetrical, as are most of the harmonies associated with it (e.g., the augmented triad). But there are many Debussyian patterns based on symmetrical structures which are not necessarily derived from whole-tone scales at all; some of these are individual events, others are combinations of events generally arranged in parallels. Characteristic are chains of triads, of seventh, ninth, or eleventh chords, or of related structures built on fourth or major seconds, arranged in pentatonic, whole-tone, diatonic, or chromatic patterns, the last-named including free, sliding chromatic shifts based on "secondary function" chords but often arrived at through parallel or sequential motion. This parallel, symmetrical (rather than contrapuntal, contrary) motion has its counterpart in the rhythmic and phrase structure, also built on parallelism and symmetry. Thus, the principle which obtains in the choice of chord and melodic line extends to the broad melodic and harmonic movement of Debussy's music and ultimately determines the larger motion and form of each piece. (See, for instance, the parallel and symmetrical structures which dominate *Jeux;* Example 3-1.)

The fine, elegant tonal imagination of Debussy is thus given a much wider and profounder field of action and expression than its apparently limited character might initially seem to suggest. In traditional tonality, the musical motion, expression, and, ultimately, structure are all inter-related functions of the unequal and fundamentally asymmetrical character of the basic material—the major-minor scales and triads, with their unequal intervals and hierarchies of motion and value. Debussy was the first composer to substitute successfully another set of values, a kind of musical thought based on symmetrical patterns and structures with a highly weakened directional motion and thus a very ambiguous sense of tonal organization. Debussy consciously exploits this ambiguity, often setting it by contrast against clear tonal, cadential statements and reinterpreting identical melodic or harmonic events in parallel, contrasting ways—somewhat in the manner of certain classical techniques but with a difference. Traditional tonal techniques, such as the sequence, function as delaying or extending devices which create secondary areas of tonal ambiguity to reinforce a bigger motion from one primary area to another; in Debussy's music, these ambiguities are built into the structure of the musical thought.

One result of this ambiguity of tonal relationships is that rhythm, phrase, dynamic, accent, and tone color are largely freed from direct dependence on tonal motion; they tend to gain an importance in the musical process almost equal to that of melody and harmony. This was an ex-

a. Four-note chromatic group filling in minor third (meas. 1-2).

Hn., harp.

b. Whole-tone harmonies, moving by major thirds (meas. 5-6).

Hn., harp, cel.

c. Major seconds in parallel motion; simultaneous,
   independent chromatic lines (meas. 25-30).

EXAMPLE 3-1. Debussy, *Jeux*. Quoted by permission of Durand & Cie, Editeurs–propriétaires, Paris.

tremely significant development, as important in a positive sense as the breakdown of the old tonality was in a negative way. The rhythmic and phrase forms, the dynamics, the articulation, and the tone color are as basic in the music of Debussy as the actual choice of pitches, or very nearly so. In a sense, the qualities of the musical ideas are often so interdependent that the various components of the sound seem to shade off into one another; that is, under certain circumstances, pitch almost functions as color, color takes the place of line (there is often a clear "rhythm" of color changes), dynamics and articulation provide rhythmic and phrase impetus, and so forth. Thus one finds individual sound patterns and even isolated sounds which seem to create their own context; they appear as conceptions which are endowed in equal part with pitch, a dynamic, accent, rhythm, and color, all inseparable and interdependent and forming the sound structures, the *ideas* of each piece. These ideas are valid, so to speak, in their own terms—for their value as sound and perhaps for their psychological effect, not for their position in a directional development or ongoing variations. They build up in relatively static structures organized in the juxtaposition of linked and parallel ideas. Tonal centers are ultimately established, not by linear motion, but out of the focusing and re-focusing of shifting, fluctuating patterns which in themselves are fluid yet unified and full of specific, identifiable character, and which combine through analogy, juxtaposition, and symmetry. An analogy might be drawn from one of Debussy's own musical "subjects": the sea, whose waves form a powerful surge of undulating motion in varying crests and troughs without necessarily any real movement underneath.

The development of Debussy's style can be traced with a great deal of clarity from the derivative, even Wagnerian sound of his early music to the final, remarkable abstract pieces of the war years. The Baudelaire songs of 1890, the String Quartet of 1893, and the *Prélude à l'après-midi d'un faune* of 1892–1894 are the first mature works; the composer's style is completely established in the *Chansons de Bilitis* and in the Verlaine songs of the period 1898–1904, the *Estampes* and *Images* for piano of 1903, 1905, and 1907, and the orchestral *La Mer* of 1903–1905 and *Images* of 1909. A still greater broadening of techniques and resources can be found in works around 1910: the *Trois Ballades de François Villon*, the two sets of *Préludes* for piano, the music for the d'Annunzio *Le Martyre de St. Sébastian*, and the ballet *Jeux*. The last works of 1915–1917—the twelve *Etudes* for piano and the sonatas for cello and piano, for flute, viola, and harp, and for violin and piano—suggest striking new directions. For the first time since the String Quartet, Debussy abandoned literary associations. In the *Etudes*, Debussy set himself quite literally a series of specifically technical-creative problems to solve, problems which lie at the very root of new musical organization and communication. In the sonatas, he similarly attacked questions of musical structure and of the organization of thought projected onto broader, simpler planes of large, neo-tonal form and intimate, precise communication.

After Debussy

The musical manner of Debussy has been widely imitated, and an attempt has been made to elevate this manner into a style or school which has, by analogy with the terminology of art history, been dubbed "impressionism." Musical impressionism seems to imply certain kinds of colorful "tone painting" based on Debussy's harmonic and melodic palette and, especially, on a range of shimmering, blended instrumental colors. What was originally a rather subtle and esoteric manner quickly became adapted to the functions of background music, partly because of the easy identification of coloristic resources, partly because the fluidity and non-assertive character of the style made it an ideally unobtrusive and psychologically apt material for dramatic accompaniment, and partly because the static ambiguity of the tonal motion made it easy to create musical materials of flexible length without assertive beginning, middle, or end.

Nevertheless, in spite of the fact that there has been—and continues to be—a good deal of Debussyism in a superficial sense, there has never been any real Debussy school. If the minor imitators and movie-music pastiches are ruled out, the entire "impressionist" movement boils down to Debussy himself, a few early works of Maurice Ravel (1875–1937), and a handful of pages in the work of a few outlanders. Ravel's early style does derive from Debussy although, in a few cases, Ravel's development seems parallel to or even in advance of Debussy. It is in his piano music, especially, and in music for the theater that Ravel's originality and independence from Debussy can be best understood. *Jeux d'eau* of 1901, *Miroirs* of 1905, and *Gaspard de la Nuit* of 1908 (all for piano), the one-act comic opera *L'Heure espagnole* of 1907, and the ballet *Daphnis et Chloé* of 1909–1911 are the works in which Ravel remains closest to Debussy and the conventional notions of "impressionism"; but, already in these pieces, the far more classical orientation of Ravel is evident. Ravel is always fastidious as to detail and closely concerned with a recognizable frame of external structure; he is involved with line, clarity of articulation, brilliant, idiomatic writing, and careful tonal organization. In the end, Ravel may be classified as a classicist, and his particular contribution found in a unique ability to combine the rich harmonic and melodic vocabulary of ninths and elevenths with free motion of parallel chords and chromatic sidesteps, all animating simple forms which are themselves the result of a new and clear sense of tonal movement.

There is scarcely another composer of note who can be described as "impressionist." Paul Dukas (1865–1935), an elegant and fastidious composer of very limited output, was influenced by Debussy, and the very prolific Florent Schmitt (1870–1958) has sometimes been classified in this way. The English composer Frederic Delius (1862–1934), who lived a good part of his life in France, evolved something of an original version of the Debussy manner, and the style is represented in America by the talented Charles Griffes (1884–1920), who died just at the moment that he was developing a personal idiom, free of Debussyism. The list is hardly longer than that; as we have seen, Debussy himself was scarcely a "Debussyiste" by the end of his life.

Nevertheless, Debussy's influence on the music of this century was incalculable, and it has hardly ended. The techniques which he evolved are most obviously in evidence in the work of a number of non-Germanic composers—most notably Vaughan Williams, but also De Falla, Bartók and Kodály, Ernest Bloch, Respighi and Puccini, one or two of the Russians —who were all in one way or another interested in establishing some kind of new tonal-modal style based on a particular local musical tradition or language which lay outside of or broke the bonds of classical tonality. For them, the new Debussyian vocabulary offered a set of expressive and formal resources within which a great variety of ideas and materials could be expanded, integrated, and made expressive in terms of a high artistic style. Also, the new free harmonic techniques could often be combined with modal melodic tradition—a fact which Debussy himself exploited and which suggested a natural way of using folk material without squeezing it into pre-cut tonal patterns.

The long-range influence of Debussy has, however, been even more profound. The disassociation of the individual sound event, the elevation of timbre and articulation to a point equal to harmony and melody, the use of constructions free from tonal patterns and based on symmetry, as well as the consequent building up of new static and associative forms are all important twentieth-century ideas which find a point of origin in the work of Debussy. In this broader sense, the French composer's influence is traceable in the developing ideas of Schoenberg, Berg, and Webern as well as of Stravinsky and Bartók; indeed, it can be found in most of the principal trends of the century and is still significant in the work of certain latter-day avant-gardists, notably Pierre Boulez.

Le Sacre du Printemps. The role of Paris as an international artistic and intellectual center in the years preceding World War I was enhanced by the presence in the French capital of a considerable number of foreign artists. Of the musicians resident in or closely associated with Paris, the Russians were the most important. Russian musical thought had, throughout the nineteenth century, maintained some independence from that of Central Europe, and the continuing vitality of older folk and liturgical traditions was a continuous challenge to classical tonality. The Russianism of "The Five" provided non-Western elements that were occasionally more than decorative; in Mussorgsky's music the Russian materials are deeply felt and penetrate to the core of the style. Mussorgsky's so-called crudities were in reality departures from the accepted Western tonal norms; even Rimsky-Korsakov could not conventionalize Mussorgsky's forms.

At the beginning of this century, Russian art was in the vanguard of European development and it continued to be so well into the Soviet period. The Stalinization of Soviet music and the subsequent insistence on a national and popular symphonic style has served to obscure the work and the very existence of an important and original group of Russian composers active in the first quarter of the century, including the remarkable Nikolay Rosslavetz (1881–1944) who anticipated aspects of twelve-tone music, and Alexander Mossolov (b. 1900), a kind of Soviet Varèse who experimented with percussion materials.

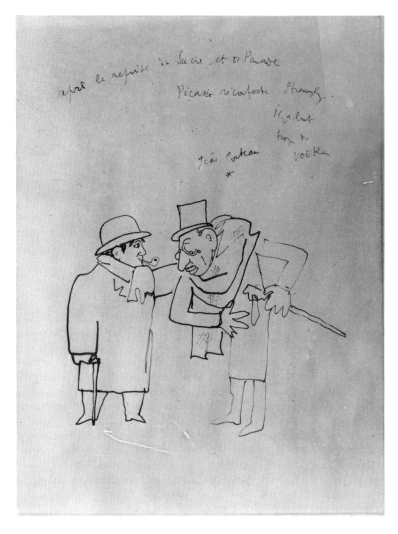

Pablo Picasso and Igor Stravinsky by Jean Cocteau. Meyer Collection, Paris. Reproduction forbidden. "After the reprise of 'Sacre' and of 'Parade' (Satie ballet for which Picasso did the decor), Picasso comforts Stravinsky. He drank too much vodka."

Stravinsky playing *Le Sacre du Printemps*, 1913. Sketch by Jean Cocteau. Meyer Collection, Paris. Reproduction forbidden.

The first Russian composer, however, to influence the course of creative musical thought was Alexander Scriabin (1872–1915). A little younger than Debussy, two years older than Schoenberg, and influenced by both, Scriabin was nonetheless a profoundly original creative mind who never quite found new forms for his profoundly new ideas. He was an excellent pianist who started out as a Chopinist and used the piano all his life as the medium for his profoundest creations.[2] He was a declared visionary, and the gradual suspension of tonality in his music was associated with a kind of post-Wagnerian chromatic mysticism. Whatever its mainsprings, his style eventually evolved into a kind of exotic modality (based on a scale of three whole steps, a minor third, and a minor second) and, finally, into a crystalline, motionless atonality built on harmonies compounded in

[2] Scriabin, who was influenced by Chopin and Liszt, was, like them, a performing musician who linked Eastern European origins with a Central European style and (to a point) French taste, to produce a series of innovations and, in the end, a style of great originality. Scriabin's influence might seem greater if we knew more about chromatic music in the Soviet Union.

fourths. Some of the early theorists of contemporary music (including Schoenberg) attempted to systematize the use of harmonic structures built in fourths by analogy with the old constructions in thirds. But the parallels are misleading and we can see today that the major "theoretical" significance of the fourth lies in the fact that, along with the minor second, it is the basic unit of a series which generates the complete tempered chromatic scale. In any case, Scriabin's use of fourths is based on symmetrical structures and clearly derived from an intensified dissonant "impressionistic" chromaticism.

Scriabin toured a great deal as a pianist and lived for periods in Paris and other parts of Western Europe, but he died before the Revolution forced the fateful split between Russian expatriate and Soviet artist. Sergei Prokofiev (1891–1953), after producing a series of highly original works based on a kind of dissonant, rhythmical, sophisticated primitivism, left (Czarist) Russia for Paris, where he elaborated a symphonic and theatrical style of considerable scope. He later went back to (Soviet) Russia to develop a lyric-symphonic popular Soviet manner. On the other hand, Stravinsky (b. 1882), who derived from Rimsky-Korsakov and started out as a purveyor of stylized Russian and Eastern exoticisms in Paris, never went back but settled in the West instead, developing a mature style which was to become the dominant influence in Western music for more than a quarter-century. Stravinsky's first important works were written under the influence of his teacher, Rimsky-Korsakov, tempered by a little Debussy and a decidedly original and volatile imagination. Only the use of orchestral color and a few piquant harmonies and rhythms amid the genteel exoticism of *L'Oiseau de feu* of 1910 and the picturesque and wry, fantastic humor of *Petrouchka* of the following year suggest what was to follow: the violence of *Le Sacre du Printemps* and the reconstruction of a new kind of tonality.

Le Sacre was completed in 1912,[3] the same year that Debussy composed his *Jeux* and Schoenberg his *Pierrot Lunaire*. Just as *Jeux* suggests the crisis of form and *Pierrot* that of harmonic and melodic organization, *Le Sacre* marks a definitive break with the old rhythm-phrase-accent structures. In Stravinsky's pivotal ballet score, rhythm and accent are clearly divorced from their old dependence on melodic and harmonic tonal organization and motion; indeed, if anything, the harmonic sense of the music is actually closely dependent on the rhythmic and accentual organization. The way things happen in *Le Sacre* is determined by the almost kinesthetic impact of violent rhythmic articulation and accents organized in asymmetrical, shifting patterns. The harmonic structures and simple melodic patterns are virtually isolated; "chords" and melodic bits appear as individual static objects; they relate to each other often only by virtue

---

[3] Stravinsky did not move to Paris until 1920, and *Le Sacre* was composed in French Switzerland, where the composer lived between 1910 and 1920. But it is with the Paris of the Russian Ballet that the work is inextricably associated.

of patterns of repetition and of shifting metrical accent. Ideas based on simple, insistent repetition gain long-range power and significance through the juxtaposition of contrasting patterns and planes and through their constant rhythmic and metrical reinterpretation. Example 3-2 shows related chord structures from *Le Sacre;* note that the opening chord of the "Danse Sacrale" is a transposition of the chord in Ex. 3-2a. These static

a. "Danses des adolescentes, " at 13 .

b. At 14 .

c. At 15 .

EXAMPLE 3-2. Stravinsky, *Le Sacre du Printemps.* Copyright 1921 by Edition Russe de Musique. Copyright assigned to Boosey and Hawkes, Inc. Reprinted by permission.

d. At 25 .

e. "Danse sacrale," beginning (original version)

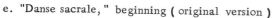

EXAMPLE 3-2 continued.

harmonic-color sounds, surrounded by equally static fragments of chromatic or modal melody, are set forth not as part of a structure in motion but through insistent repetition and rhythmic-accentual displacement.

Everything in *Le Sacre* is asserted, everything is given by the piece itself; nothing falls into place naturally or by expectation. This is a piece of high artifice in the best sense; the idea that it is a "primitive" work seems to be due—aside from the obvious fact of the subject matter of the ballet—to the quality of disassociated insistence which, combined with the striking use of chordal, noncontrapuntal dissonance, produces an effect of arbitrary, motionless, elemental power. In actual fact, every gesture is carefully calculated and the dynamic articulation of the whole carefully worked. *Le Sacre* is less obviously "atonal" and seemingly more primitive than corresponding Viennese works only because it is not linear-chromatic. In fact, it at once presents and creatively resolves very complex psychological and musical problems of disassociated ideas, and of block structure built in layers and realized, not through the old contained use of power to produce motion, but from the complete and explosive rhythmic release of very confined and volatile musical energies. For Stravinsky, *Le Sacre* was, in many ways, a beginning, middle, and end; he quickly went on to other things. Nevertheless, many of Stravinsky's characteristic and fundamental techniques first appear in *Le Sacre*. Most important,

Le Sacre is a music which takes shape, not through the extension of line and counterpoint, but through the juxtaposition of static levels of sound and statement, dividing up and punctuating psychological time with rhythmic and accentual statement, articulation, and interpretation.

Bibliography

For the intellectual climate in late nineteenth-century France, see A. G. Lehmann, *The Symbolist Aesthetic in France*, Oxford, 1950. There are books in English on Satie and Ravel by Rollo W. Meyers (London, 1948, 1960). The major study on Debussy in English is Edward Lockspeiser's two-volume work (London, 1962, 1964); The basic French sources are the writings of Léon Vallas; one work in English translation is *The Theories of Debussy*, London, 1929. See also Debussy's own "Monsieur Croche" articles translated and reprinted in the *Three Classics* volume cited in the bibliography for Chapter 2. For one view of the relationship between Debussy and Ravel see Charles Rosen's "Where Ravel Ends and Debussy Begins" in the May, 1959 issue of *High Fidelity* magazine. For modern views of Debussy's importance see *Debussy et l'évolution de la musique au 20e siècle* (ed. Edith Weber, Paris, 1965). A modern analysis of *Jeux*, by Herbert Eimert, appears in Vol. 5 of the journal *Die Reihe*.

For the early works of Stravinsky and the background of *Le Sacre du Printemps* see especially Stravinsky's own *Chronicles of My Life*, London, 1936, and the many references in the four volumes of conversations with Robert Craft: *Conversations With Igor Stravinsky, Memories and Commentaries, Expositions and Developments, Dialogues and a Diary* (Garden City, N.Y., 1959, 1960, 1962, 1963); additional Stravinsky bibliography appears at the end of Chapter 5. A modern view of *Le Sacre* by Pierre Boulez appears in *Musique Russe*, v. 1, ed. P. Souvtchinsky (Paris 1953).

4

The Revolution: Vienna

At the turn of the twentieth century, Paris had only one rival as the capital of Europe: Vienna, still the seat of the Austro-Hungarian Empire and still a cultural crossroads. Vienna had once been the meeting place of the musical North and South, where the contrapuntal and instrumental techniques of the Germans mingled with the operatic and instrumental styles of Italy; the child of that Viennese marriage was the classical symphony. At the opening of this century, Vienna—the city of Freud and Schnitzler, of the Secessionist movement and Gustav Mahler—was to become the center of the transformation of that very classical tonality which had produced some of her greatest musical achievements.

The author of that transformation, Arnold Schoenberg, was born in

Vienna in 1874. Schoenberg was essentially self-taught and always remained outside the powerful Vienna musical "establishment," but he entirely mastered traditional technique and he remained all his life involved in the study and teaching, not only of the classical disciplines, but of the profoundest and most universal aspects of the tradition. Schoenberg's starting point was, of course, Wagner—specifically the Wagner of *Tristan* and *Parsifal*—but his real intellectual antecedents were Bach, Beethoven, and Brahms. He began with the Wagnerian chromatic vocabulary, but from the start, his basic concerns were with that intellectual integrity and totality of conception which—as he himself did so much to show—were basic to the classical tradition. Schoenberg's music is steeped in contrapuntal principles, in notions of the complex interrelationships between the vertical and the horizontal, and in concepts of total form, and it is through these ideas, older and more universal than classical tonality itself, that we can understand his development. He was also a thorough-going Hegelian; that is, he believed that music, like all aspects of human life, is part of a process of change and that there are universal and inevitable principles which control history and historical change. For Schoenberg the classical tradition of form—the concept of an all-pervasive intellectual organization—represented a universal principle, while the development of chromaticism represented a principle of change and evolution. The growth of equal temperament, chromaticism, and modulation made possible the historical rise of functional tonality in the seventeenth and eighteenth centuries and destroyed it in the twentieth; thus tonality contained within itself from the start the seed of its own destruction.

Schoenberg's *Verklärte Nacht* of 1899—originally written for string sextet, later recast for string orchestra—and his massive *Gurrelieder* of 1900–1901 (orchestrated in 1910), for soloists, chorus, and large orchestra, are still, in spite of their great originality, within the Wagnerian orbit. The works of the years 1902–1907—including the symphonic poem *Pelleas und Melisande* (after Maeterlinck and written at about the time that Debussy completed his operatic version), the First String Quartet in D minor, and the *Kammersinfonie*—show a steady but marked expansion of chromatic and contrapuntal techniques with the effect of delaying tonal resolution over longer and longer periods. This is particularly true of the Chamber Symphony, in which whole-tone patterns and melodic and harmonic constructions in fourths appear. These techniques, related to those of Debussy, represent aspects of the total chromatic material: adjacent whole-tone scales as well as cycles of fourths will generate the complete chromatic gamut; also, half-step, whole-tone, and fourth patterns have important characteristics of symmetry which distinguish them from the unbalanced, "hierarchical" structures of major-minor triads and scales. But Schoenberg was never primarily interested in working out the harmonic implications of these kinds of structures; his instinct (later formalized) was to seek out the meaning of harmonic structures in their relationship to line, and the technique of most of his later music (with some exceptions) is based on complex, chromatic, contrapuntal thinking with motivic and, increasingly, intervallic construction carried out within smaller and smaller revolutions of the total chromatic cycle. The Second String Quartet (completed 1908) shows the germ of the process within a single work; the composition begins well within the bounds of a contrapuntal, chromatic tonality, organized thematically, and then proceeds towards a linear chromaticism in which motives and intervals assume the structural force exerted formerly by tonal expectation and function.

In the work which followed, the *Three Piano Pieces*, Op. 11 (completed 1909), the new non-tonal motivic chromaticism is completely dominant. The opening phrases still have a thematic function but they also form fundamental sound matter which accounts for a good deal of what happens in the piece (Example 4-1). Thus the interval of a major third with a half step inside or outside ("X") and the outline of a tritone with adjacent whole or half steps ("Y" and "Z") form basic harmonic as well as melodic structures; the piece is saturated with the characteristic sound of these intervals (including, of course, their closely associated "inversional" forms such as major sevenths, etc.). Furthermore, long-range motion not only outlines characteristic intervals (see, for example, the opening melodic phrase which outlines B-F–natural-E; i.e. tritone–half step) but fills in significant segments of the chromatic scale. The use of intervallic relationship in the small is thus taken up in a more fundamental associative musical motion.[1] There is, of course, simple thematic statement and development. But this must now function entirely without the aid of tonal motion, support, or superstructure. For the first time, every sound, every interval, every event has a unique and independent value, free of the hierarchies of tonal discourse—and equally free of the meanings formerly invested in them. Thematic development remains, but totally abstracted from its old contexts. This was not enough for Schoenberg; it was necessary for him to transform the entire musical material so that the old balance and interaction between all aspects of the musical matter and discourse were restored in some new artistic synthesis. His solution, right from the start, was to affirm a basic unity between linear and vertical events and to assert (this is not merely assumed but aggressively asserted by the music) the fundamental identity of the individual elements of the tempered, chromatic scale.

The piano pieces of Op. 11 were followed by a series of important works including the song cycle from Stefan Georg's "Book of the Hanging Gardens" (Op. 15, begun in 1907); the *Five Orchestral Pieces*, Op. 16, of 1909; the operas *Erwartung* and *Die Glückliche Hand* of 1909 and 1913; the *Six Little Piano Pieces*, Op. 19 (1911), *Herzgewächse* for soprano, celesta, harmonium, and harp, Op. 20 (also 1911); *Pierrot Lunaire*, Op. 21, of 1912; and the *Four Orchestral Songs*, Op. 22, of 1913–1916. In

---

[1] These techniques were, of course, later formally synthesized by Schoenberg in the "twelve-tone" method or system.

a. Interval structures.

b. Opening Measures.

EXAMPLE 4-1. Schoenberg, *Three Piano Pieces*, Op. 11; No. 1. Quoted by permission of Mrs. Gertrud Schoenberg and Universal Edition.

all of these works, chromatic motion functions without tonal controls to indicate direction or to set up long-range relationships. There is a definite impulse towards the highest chromatic density, and as a result, a strong tendency towards the constant and repeated use of all twelve notes on an even and revolving basis. The pieces hold together not only through the extended use of motives in the thematic sense but through the play of distinctive pitch combinations which give characteristic sound and shape to each work. The writing is contrapuntally conceived; but harmonic, articulative, timbral, and rhythmic statement may all be decisive in the character of the ideas and their organization. Thus, although we now see that the rhythmic and phrase structures of these works come out of their immediate late-tonal predecessors, these structures are not governed by a more basic (tonal) impulse but themselves give motion to the music.[2] Similarly, dynamics, accent, articulation, and coloration are indicated with unprecedented exactness and detail; nothing could be assumed any more from context; every event and every aspect of every event had a new and independent meaning. Each of the pieces sets forth its own musical, expressive, and formal premises; every event is unique; and each piece becomes the particular development and realization of unique and independent events interrelating through a unique set of premises.

Each of these works represents some very particular discoveries and explorations of new and distinctive aspects of musical experience. Some of these experiences are timbral; there is an enormous expansion of instrumental and orchestral technique in these works (as in comparable works of Berg and Webern) which is in every way parallel to the expansion of materials and resources in the other musical domains. Instrumental colors formerly considered exceptional (mutes, *sul ponticello*, harmonics, flutter-tonguing, etc.) are normal here, and techniques formerly of great rarity (*col legno battuto* and *tratto*, harmonics on the piano, etc.) are common. Instruments are used in extreme and unusual registers and dynamic levels, while an enormous variety of instrumental combinations are employed. The movement of the *Five Orchestral Pieces* entitled "Farben" is realized completely in terms of a series of subtle harmonic and timbral changes rung on a chordal structure. In the monodrama *Erwartung*, Schoenberg even abandons thematic-motivic structure in order to create a psychological-dramatic form based on on-going chromatic line, on an articulation of changing intensities, and on an athematic intervallic structure; the kaleidoscopic orchestral treatment—in a consistent state of flux—is used to project a single, long psychological form and motion. Yet, at the same time, in the unfinished orchestral pieces of 1909, Schoenberg, like Webern, used an entirely different concept of the orchestra as an interweaving of solo sounds used to project miniature form. Conversely, the sound of a solo instrument is "scored" in timbral terms in a work like the *Six Little Piano Pieces*, Op. 19—studies in concise, aphoristic expression, each one of which articulates some brief, precise aspect of the chromatic experience.

Nearly all of the techniques of Schoenberg's early period (including even brief reminiscences of tonality) are present in his *Pierrot Lunaire*, twenty-one poems by Albert Giraud in a German translation, set for *Sprechstimme* and chamber ensemble. Characteristically, the work is severely patterned in a symmetrical and prophetically serialized arrangement: the poems, strict *rondeaux*, are grouped in three sets of seven each, and the chamber instrumentation is varied from song to song to obtain

---

[2] This is one reason why this aspect of this music, which today seems the most related to the past, appeared for a long time as the most difficult and impenetrable.

maximum differentiation. Motivic and intervallic constructions of every kind are used, incorporated into complex linear textures employing some of the classical canonic forms, sometimes closely organized, sometimes free. The vocal line, for the most part, is not actually sung but declaimed according to the *Sprechstimme* or "speech-song" technique first used by Schoenberg in his *Gurrelieder:* fixed pitches are indicated but the vocalist is directed to follow the curve of the notated line in a manner that stands somewhere between song and speech. These songs—like many early works of Schoenberg—show an exceptional sensitivity to texture, and indeed the most basic and compelling formal aspect of the composition is its underlying organization in fluid, flashing, chromatic textures set into patterns of great severity and profundity.

It is not insignificant that the early pivotal works of Debussy, Stravinsky, and Schoenberg were involved with some kind of theatrical or literary statement; in Schoenberg's case, we can easily infer the importance of "expressive intent" in his chromatic revolution. But none of the great innovators of the twentieth century—least of all Schoenberg—was exclusively concerned with expressive detail, and the key problem was how to derive meaningful form out of the new materials generated by an expressive upheaval. Schoenberg was eventually to solve this problem in a characteristic and significant way, but in the meantime, he devised a series of interim solutions which grew organically out of a remarkable series of new materials and new experiences. It is interesting to note, in the light of our latter-day new music—as it has emerged from a strict and intellectual serialism derived from the later work of Schoenberg and Webern —that the earlier explorations and approaches to the communication of a new world of free, flexible, and invented imagination seem more remarkable and meaningful than ever.

Berg and Webern

Schoenberg was the only one of the major composers of the early part of the century to have had important pupils, and two of these, Alban Berg (1885–1935) and Anton Webern (1883–1945), have a major place in the development of modern creative ideas. Convenient historical niches have been found for both: Berg has been described as an instinctual lyricist whose music links with tradition, while Webern has been seen as the intellectual, numerical abstractionist and the unrecognized avant-garde prophet. Like most such generalizations, these labels cover a rich reality with a thin tissue of truths. Over half of Webern's output is vocal, for example, and many aspects of his work are a deliberate re-casting of traditional patterns in a new aphoristic style often conceived in terms of an underlying lyricism. In certain ways, Berg's music is actually more independent of tradition. It is true that Berg did not take up Schoenberg's twelve-tone idea with as much enthusiasm as Webern, but on the other hand, Berg was the most numerologically inclined of the three; his works are full of the most elaborate—often arbitrary—number sequences, precise and fearful symmetries carried out in every dimension and domain. Berg was the kind of "instinctualist" who placed great faith in elaborate, mystical, and arbitrary systems.

Alban Berg by Franz Rederer. Reproduced by permission of the Music Division of The New York Public Library.

Portrait of Anton Webern by Oskar Kokoschka. Reproduced by permission of Annie Knize.

Berg's early songs and his Piano Sonata, Op. 1 (1906–1908), come out of a post-Wagnerian tradition touched by Debussy and the contrapuntal genius of Schoenberg. The Sonata, with its chromatic lines pulsing in a continual ebb and flow, is, by courtesy, tonal, but the shifting Scriabin-esque harmonic impact of lines never articulates an organic tonal structure with any clarity. The piece resolves itself on its B minor point of tonal departure, but the resolution is imposed. The real structure of the piece—like that of the related String Quartet, Op. 3—is a complex of unresolved motions deriving from an inner web of motives and motivic intervals which never seem to articulate or be articulated by the on-going harmonic flux. In a sense, these were the problems and contradictions with which Berg was to wrestle all his life; in the end, he was able to deal with them by recognizing the contradiction and building his music on the very concept of conflict and opposition.

The Four Songs, Op. 2, written between 1907 and 1909, derive from the late-romantic lied tradition and from Wagnerian harmony tinged with not a little Debussy; yet the mixture is personal, and in the end, it brings Berg close to an expressive atonality. The *"Altenberg" Lieder*, Op. 4, for soprano and orchestra (1912), are the first fully mature works in consistency and quality of invention and expression; they have Berg's characteristically intense linear-melodic style combined with his remarkable sense of color as an organic part of the conception. Berg's pieces grow out of an interplay between line (the concept of line and phrase which comes out of the tradition) and the play of color and texture (the most original and far-reaching aspect of his work); it is in this sense that the forms are organic and original.

Both the Clarinet and Piano Pieces, Op. 5 (1913), and the Three Orchestral Pieces, Op. 6 (1913–14), achieve expressive form through a complex interplay of line, register, color, and texture. Op. 5 is a set of miniatures, closely related to contemporaneous pieces by Schoenberg and Webern. The pieces of Op. 6 are at the opposite extreme in scope and specific gravity, although their enormous contrapuntal density ends up by communicating analogous structures made out of timbre and sonority as well as line. The first movement is an early and exceptional example of a piece framed in percussion sound (but see Webern's Op. 6, No. 4); and the long, contrapuntal pile-up of the march-like third movement is built up in accumulations of orchestral sound. All of these works depend in great part on the effect of a complex irresolution. The Piano Sonata is virtually the last word in chromatic tonality, built up in shifting, oscillating, ambiguous harmonic structures which, nevertheless, are still presumed to have tonal and directional functions. In the following works, tonal functions persist only obliquely, and in the Op. 6 pieces, ideas are expressed in dense, insistent lines weighted down with a tremendous expressive baggage and almost impossible to clarify in performance. At times, Berg seems actually to be composing in textures and densities whose inner detail is complex, very free and variable, and not at all clearly defined aurally. The music is formed through a process of accumulation; Berg replaces the directional movement of tonality with a new and simpler kind of directionality based on the accumulation of tension and texture.

In *Wozzeck*, written between 1914 and 1921, Berg used the whole range of techniques found in his early works but now enormously expanded by the simultaneous use of a complex of dramatic, literary, and classical musical forms. Berg arranged a remarkable series of fragments by Georg Büchner into a kaleidoscopic libretto about a wretched army orderly who kills his unfaithful mistress and drowns himself. *Wozzeck* is, from one point of view, a social document cast in the theatrical and musical idiom of the early part of the century known as "expressionism." But on a profounder level, *Wozzeck* is about the human condition. The seemingly brutalized Wozzeck is a character of a certain grandeur; a visionary who, in his essential uniqueness and humanity, has just what the other characters lack—a certain natural nobility. Similarly, the music has a range and grandeur even in the almost touching sordidness and literalness of certain details. The intentionally vulgarized stage music stands next to a whole series of chamber and symphonic patterns which are sketched out underneath. Berg has imposed a classical shape or procedure on each of the fifteen scenes, and the larger forms of the acts are arranged as a series of interconnected formal patterns and symmetries; even in small details, number and system play a surprisingly decisive role. Berg, whose musical style was complex, free, and fluid, set himself rigid frameworks as if to give his musical imagination something solid from which to push off. In a sense, these rigid patterns serve something of the same function (on a simpler level, to be sure) as the twelve-tone conception in Schoenberg's later work. *Wozzeck* is, of course, in no sense twelve-tone—it was completed before Schoenberg's first twelve-tone pieces—but it does contain a prominent theme made up of all twelve notes (so does Strauss' *Also sprach Zarathustra*) and there is often a striking tendency towards a total chromatic density. Indeed, the techniques run from simple triadic writing to the most intense "atonality," from *Sprechstimme* to lyric line, from diatonic melody to chromatic parlando, from chamber-ensemble counterpoint to broad orchestral strokes, from complex, busy motion to static intensity, from isolated, aphoristic punctuation to broad on-going development. There are sonata and variation forms, *Leitmotiv* development, bits of popular song, small closed forms, and big, open psychological ones that ultimately determine the shape of the whole. The famous orchestral interlude that precedes the final scene takes on the function of summation; it universalizes the trivial and sordid tragedy. *Wozzeck* thus becomes more than a proletarian tragedy and more than the cumulative effect of a series of expressive and immediately comprehensible musical strokes. It remains the only post-Wagnerian, post-tonal work written in a heavily dissonant, chromatic style which has had a consistent theatrical success, and it remains the classic example of chromatic, "atonal" style combined with classical, closed forms applied, uniquely and with great psychological validity, to a modern, intense, dramatic expression.

Whereas Berg expanded Schoenberg's chromatic vision into large forms, dependent on tradition and psychological insight, Webern worked almost from the first in an opposite direction—towards the isolation of the single event, the disassociation of adjacent events into the context of the total interrelationship of the whole. Webern is at once the simplest and the most difficult of composers: the most and least intellectual, the easiest to take apart yet the hardest to follow, the most esoteric yet the most comprehensible, the most classical yet the most advanced, the most individual and personal yet the most influential and widely imitated. It is the simplicity of Webern's esthetic which explains the paradoxes—Webern's music consists of few notes set forth over a very short period of time; he reduced the problem of expressive form to the fact of the isolated, individual event and in so doing made every interpretation of the single event a possible one. It is from this point of view that Webern can be said to have re-invigorated a "classical" view of form while, at the same time, completed the destruction of tonal thinking.

Webern achieved his mature style very quickly, and his later development took place almost entirely within the narrow limits of his personal esthetic of clarity and concision. His principle is that of maximum variety within an extremely tight and condensed unity. Theme, development, and structural motion and relationship appear as a single sound or event. The unit is the interval between adjacent or simultaneous sounds, isolated, carefully defined, and packed with the maximum possible expressive and intellectual content. This concept of the interval had, even before the formulation of twelve-tone principles, the notion of succession as its fundamental principle. This linear-melodic basis to Webern's music—harmonic structure becomes a function of the simultaneity of musical events whose origin can be found in linear succession—is reflected in the fact that over half of his works are vocal; among the early compositions, Op. 2, 3, 4, 8, 12, 13, 14, and 15 are for voices. All of these works employ traditional pitched singing—Webern never used *Sprechstimme*—and most of them use solo voices with piano and instruments in the lied tradition.

Webern's detached, intense way of building up phrases by linking isolated tones and intervals and relating small groups of "melodic" tones also carries over into his early instrumental pieces as a way of unfolding very abstract and static formal conceptions in real time. These works are characterized by intense brevity, a pure, even lyric, quality, and a careful constructed unity. The pitch successions, whether isolated or grouped in small cells, form a series of points which tend to fill up a distinct and very carefully defined musical space. Thus a succession will be divided between various registers and in and between various instruments and instrumental groupings. Colors and registers come to form a succession of equal importance to that of the pitches themselves, and all elements are closely grouped in clear and close relationships.

Already in the *Five Movements* for string quartet, Op. 5, of 1909, Webern applied elaborate principles of complex unity within a vastly restricted space. The *Six Pieces*, Op. 6, constitute a comparatively large work for a comparatively large orchestra, but the other works written in 1910 and after turn again towards an intense miniaturization: *Four Pieces* for violin and piano, Op. 7; *Six Bagatelles* for string quartet, Op. 9;

Five Pieces for Orchestra, Op. 10; *Three Small Pieces* for cello and piano, Op. 11. There is, to be sure, more than a trace of late-romantic statement still remaining—Mahler in an atonal nutshell! Some of the movements of Op. 5, 6, and 10 are comparatively large in scope and even the briefest gestures are full of intense, expressionist-romantic *Angst;* indeed, the concentration and the intensity of the concentration itself are a result of the enormous, unreleased energies inherent in the laconic ideas and terse forms.

In this music there is a kind of "maximization of the minimum": an intentionally limited collection of pitches, registers, colors, rhythms, accents, and articulations is revealed in its greatest possible variety. Portions of the complete chromatic gamut are filled in by half-steps (or, by the analogy of octave equivalence, by major sevenths and minor ninths) or, secondarily, by short figures arranged in whole steps, thirds and sixths; a good example of this is the first of the *Bagatelles,* Op. 9. The single event becomes striking, and most significantly, the single repetition, identity, or association becomes crucial; perhaps the most extreme example here is the Op. 11, three movements in a bare handful of measures, a few tiny gestures, mere seconds of isolated sound emerging briefly from the silence that becomes, for Webern, a basic condition of musical experience. The fourth piece of Op. 10 consists of six measures with only forty-eight separate note indications, about half of which are repeated notes (Example 4-2). There are slightly more than two revolutions of the total chromatic cycle, with miniature phrases of six, four, two, and five notes set among brief chordal structures and repeated notes. The opening harp sonority— G–flat, D–flat, F—is recapitulated in the fourth and fifth measures by the harp, clarinet, and celesta with the addition of another three harmonic elements—B, E, C—a rearrangement and inverted transposition of a companion structure. This same figure also appears melodically in the mandolin (simultaneously with the harp chord) as the A–flat, G, and E–flat of the opening phrase. The mandolin phrase also contains secondary elements of great importance pivoted around the tritone (whole step and a tritone, tritone and a half step); the nine notes of the mandolin and harp fill the chromatic space between C and A–flat. The next phrases, which begin by filling out the missing B–flat, A, and B, center on tritones with the attached whole or half-step; i.e., the opening three notes of the trumpet phrase which are an arrangement and transposition of the opening mandolin notes; the final D of the trumpet phrase and the two notes of the trombone phrase are an arrangement of the second through fourth notes of the mandolin phrase. Similarly, the following F–sharp in the harp and the C-D–flat trill in the clarinet as well as the subsequent E-F in the celesta and B in the mandolin (the same B-F relationship that began the trumpet phrase, now associated through timbre with the opening) are related figures. The final violin phrase beginning minor seventh (= whole step), tritone is a synthesis of all of the basic elements of the opening.

a. Interval structures.

b. Reduced score.

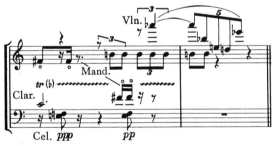

EXAMPLE 4-2. Webern, *Five Pieces for Orchestra*, Op. 10, No. 4. Quoted by permission of Universal Edition.

Webern did not pursue this line any further for a number of years; in the rest of his early period, up through his first twelve-tone works, he returned to vocal and polyphonic forms. Between 1915 and 1927—in his Op. 12 to Op. 19—he wrote exclusively for solo voices with instruments, recreating, often with considerable complexity, the forms of the polyphonic lied[3] in terms of expressive chromatic ideas and a dense, carefully

---

[3] It should be remembered that Webern was a trained musicologist whose doctoral dissertation, written under the guidance of Guido Adler, was on music by the Renaissance composer Heinrich Isaac (ca. 1450–1517).

controlled dissonant counterpoint. Webern's "historical" contribution was certainly his elaboration—and eventually refinement and systemization—of techniques of construction through the isolation of the individual event and the tightly bound relationship of pitch, duration, intensity, and color, all expressed in terms of the maximum differentiation within the most minimal, economic sequence of events in the briefest, most compressed structural time span. But Webern, like Berg, had first to follow Schoenberg in the reconstruction of a complex counterpoint based on the classical relationships but systematically chromatic and free of tonal implications. This symmetrical, chromatic, complex polyphony was, of course, to provide the basis for the twelve-tone consolidation to follow.

Bibliography

For the background on this important period, see the Schoenberg writings already mentioned as well as the recently issued letters (New York, 1965). The new translation of Willi Reich's Berg biography (New York, 1965) contains articles by Berg himself on Schoenberg and on "atonality" which are important documents of the period. Webern's *Path to New Music* (tr. Bryn Mawr, Pa., 1963) consists of transcriptions of lectures given during the "twelve-tone period," but many of the ideas can be traced back to Schoenberg's teaching and the activity of the Schoenberg circle in Vienna before World War I. For specific treatment of an individual work, see George Perle's article on *Pierrot Lunaire* in the Curt Sachs commemorative volume *The Commonwealth of Music* (New York, 1965). Perle's *Serial Composition and Atonality* (Berkeley and Los Angeles, 1962) and the Webern issue of *Die Reihe* (No. 2) contain specific discussions of pre-twelve-tone works. Walter Kolneder's *Anton Webern* guide (Roden Kirchen, 1961) discusses all of the early works. For this period, see also the other general works on Schoenberg, Berg, and Webern listed at the end of Chapter 10.

PART THREE

The
New
Tonalities

5

Stravinsky and Neo-Classicism

The effective result of the new musical developments everywhere in the early years of the century has been the weakening or the destruction of the accepted implications of traditional functional tonality. The cumulative effect, not only of the work of the "atonal" Viennese but of Debussy, of Strauss's *Elektra* and *Salome*, of *Le Sacre du Printemps*, of the early works of Bartók and the folklorists, and of a dozen lesser developments, has so permeated our musical consciousness that, except in certain very limited areas of folk and popular music, the old tonal way of thinking is no longer operative. Even in popular and light jazz forms, where triadic tonality is still a dominant feature, we accept the triad with the added sixth, even the added seventh, as a consonance, and contrapuntal voice-leading has been replaced by parallel harmonic structures including chains of unresolved sevenths and ninths; only the diatonic, four-measure melodic structures continue to reflect the strong, functional hierarchies of the old tonal music.

In the more complex and serious forms of jazz as well as in nearly every form of concert and operatic music—even the most conservative— the old tonal forms can no longer be taken for granted, and they have often been totally replaced by some kind of *new* tonal conception. Of the major figures who participated in the tonal revolutions before the First World War, only Strauss backed away, first into a kind of proto-neo-classicism and later into a quiet absorption with traditional techniques and forms. Debussy, at the time of his death, was on the verge of creating new tonal forms; in fact, such new forms and techniques came into existence within a few years of the end of World War I. All of these were synthetic; none depended on traditional tonal functions, but instead synthesized anew—even from piece to piece—their tonal structures. To put it another way, the tonal works of the past had been specific instances of processes that can be generalized; the new tonal works established their general processes as part of their individual creative statement.

A large body of the new tonal music, centered on the work of Igor Stravinsky, has been known as "neo-classical"; a more logical and more inclusive term might be "neo-tonal." Much of this music has been concerned with forms and materials derived from the classical tradition, but a great part of it also derives from an earlier or a more recent past or no particular past at all. For Stravinsky himself, the uses of the past are very significant; but restrictive and essentially polemical terms like "neo-classicism" cannot serve to indicate the range of Stravinsky's "past"—from Dufay and Isaac to Tchaikovsky and Webern—or the essential interiorization of that past, radically transformed into something new and essentially Stravinskyian. The essence of Stravinskyian "neo-classicism" lies in the thorough renovation of classical form achieved through a new and creative rebuilding of tonal practice independent of the traditional functions which had first established those forms.

After the first performance of Le Sacre in 1913 with its famous *succès de scandale*, Stravinsky returned to an unfinished theatre work, his opera Le Rossignol, which he completed in a manner markedly at variance with the original Debussy-and-Rimsky-Korsakov conception. Stravinsky could not return to the colorful semi-tonal world of the opening after the experience of Le Sacre, but a generalized tonal sense still seems to linger in the much more spare and dissonant character of the later parts of the opera. More significantly, however, Stravinsky composed a number of short instrumental and instrumental-vocal works between 1912 and 1920—two sets of pieces for piano four-hands, two works for string quartet, three pieces for solo clarinet, sets of songs for voice and instruments— which correspond roughly with the slightly earlier tendencies towards miniaturization in the music of Schoenberg and Webern. These neglected pieces are interesting because they employ tiny bits of the gigantesque, dissonant vocabulary of *Le Sacre* in brief, aphoristic forms based on nearly motionless ostinati. This tendency towards clear, static, ostinato-based forms is also clearly evident in the last two works based largely on Russian materials: the burlesque opera *Renard* of 1916–1917 and the "choreographic scenes," *Les Noces*, written between 1914 and 1917 but given its final and characteristic instrumental setting (four pianos and percussion) only in 1923. Both of these works use a high degree of static "color" dissonance combined with and set off from diatonic, "neo-Russian" melodic ideas. Even a cursory glance at *Le Sacre* will reveal that these techniques are actually already present in that score, but they are fully realized in *Les Noces*. *Les Noces* is the first of Stravinsky's works to re-establish an ancient and thorough-going tonal principle—tonality by assertion. These remarkable choral sketches of a Russian peasant wedding employ a simple yet effective melodic technique which juxtaposes brief melodic motives with ornamented figures and insistent choral chants, all set in cyclical patterns of repetition turning around one or two insistent pitches. The ritualistic quality of this writing, much enhanced by the remarkable piano-and-percussion orchestration, is further emphasized by a basic structural technique of juxtaposition of alternating and contrasting static layers of sound patterns. This technique, already present in *Le Sacre*, is the basis for the so-called "additive" construction which Stravinsky was to use throughout his life—big building-blocks of sounds and sound patterns, often based on static ostinati, set against one another in repetitive, alternating cycles which, although assertive, and unyielding in nature, gain vitality and even a sense of motion by being constantly reinterpreted in shifting overlaps of accent, rhythm, meter, and phrase.

Les Noces is one of many Stravinsky works which proved a source of inspiration to other composers but not—except in the basic ways suggested above—to Stravinsky himself. Stravinsky's next work, *L'Histoire du soldat* (1918), uses Russian folklore, but it contains few musical Russianisms;[1] up-to-date popular, dance, and jazz materials are enclosed in small forms. *L'Histoire* was conceived for a small travelling theater and it employs a narrator, mimed or danced action, and an ensemble of seven instruments including an important percussion part.[2] It is, in effect, the first of Stravinsky's "neo-classic" pieces, although in fact it contains nothing more classical than a pair of off-key chorales, a few simple, closed (really dance) forms, and a dependence on the triad (used as an articulative rather than classical tonal device). Nevertheless *L'Histoire* is the prototype for later "neo-classical" works in its references to other music, its spare but vigorous lines and colors, its shifting rhythmic and accentual

---

[1] The recurring three-note cadential phrase in the violin solo is very close to one in the recently popular Russian song "Moscow Nights"; a common source would be suggested.

[2] The musicians are to be visible; they play roles equal to those of the other performers.

organization, its use of small closed forms, its ironic wit, and its method of achieving tonal centers of gravity through assertion and juxtaposition.

Stravinsky's "neo-classic" period is generally dated from 1919, the year of the ballet *Pulcinella*, after Pergolesi. To the extent that material by Pergolesi (or whoever really wrote the music Stravinsky used as source material) actually appears, the work might be said to be tonal in the old way. Heard in these terms, *Pulcinella* becomes an eccentric set of arrangements of and intrusions on eighteenth-century style. But it is nothing of the sort, of course; Pergolesi has been transformed at every moment into something quite new. The baroque progressions are no longer representatives of a musical direction and motion; they are literally sound objects or blocks of sound which gain new meanings from new contexts. A progression or melodic pattern may begin from the middle, so to speak, or stop at some point short of a satisfactory "resolution"; such patterns are set into the typical overlapping cycles of repetition with shifting accents and metrical values; and all of this is reinforced by a clear and brilliant if restrained orchestration in which color functions analogously to rhythm and phrase.

Almost simultaneously with this derivative and "neo-classical" work, Stravinsky composed the most original and independent of his instrumental compositions, the *Symphonies of Wind Instruments* of 1920. This important if neglected work, dedicated to the memory of Debussy, is as unclassical as it is un-Debussyesque (although perhaps it owes something to both the great tradition and to the work of the French master in its absolute clarity and its originality of form, which moves from one block sonority to another through the juxtaposition of static rhythm and texture). Again, this work—although it looks back and ahead—suggests a development and a direction which Stravinsky himself never followed directly; it is, like many Stravinsky works, typical of itself.

Stravinsky's other instrumental compositions of this period show a marked tendency to develop the kind of rhythmic and harmonic vitality within closed, static forms already found in *L'Histoire:* the *Ragtime* for eleven instruments of 1918 and the *Piano Rag-Music* of 1920, the remarkable *Five-Fingers* piano pieces (whose melodies turn out to be simple permutations of *Le Sacre*-like themes), the *Three Pieces* for solo clarinet of 1919 and the *Concertino* for string quartet of 1920, the *Suite* for chamber orchestra of 1921, the fine *Piano Sonata* of 1922, the important *Octet* for winds of 1923, the *Concerto* for piano and winds of 1924, and the *Sérénade en La* for piano of 1925 move almost step by step towards the re-establishment of tonal form without a single instance of traditional tonal structure.

Parody is a word that can be used in reference to these works if the term is understood in its original sense, not necessarily implying satire. Parody technique—that is, the use and transformation of pre-existing material—was a recognized way of writing music during the Renaissance, and much more recently, similar ideas can be found in the other arts: the use of Homeric materials in James Joyce, the quotes and references in T. S. Eliot, Picasso's paintings after Delacroix. Stravinsky's esthetic is, to some extent, that of art removed to the second degree; that is, art about art or, more to the point, about the experience of art. Stravinsky's own musical experience—never limited merely to the so-called "Classical" period —is the subject matter, taken in hand and transformed with the most careful and brilliant art and artifice; the entire range of musical experience, Renaissance to ragtime, is the material for a new and entirely contemporary commentary, sometimes witty, sometimes merely elegant and decorative, sometimes kinetic and "tangible" in its rhythmic pulse, sometimes concerned with formal patternings, often dealing at a deeper level with very real problems of expressive structure and communication.

Through it all, Stravinsky is never anything less than precise. This very precision and the clarity and dryness of his style, taken in conjunction with certain polemical remarks by the composer himself, have led to the facile conclusion that Stravinsky's music is "inexpressive" (apparently in contradistinction not only to the romantic tradition, but also to the contemporary Viennese "expressionists"); it is, supposedly, intended to "express" or communicate nothing at all. Stravinsky was largely responsible for the introduction of what we might call the "cabinet-maker" theory of the composer's role in society: the composer, like his colleague the joiner, creates beautiful things that have no more or less meaning than the beautiful curve on the leg of a fine chair. A chair, of course, has a function (and the curve may express something about that function); thus to some extent Stravinsky, and to a larger extent Hindemith and others, attempted to re-establish music as a "functional" art (just as they attempted to construct new tonalities with new musical hierarchies or "functions"). Nevertheless, Stravinsky's art is by no means exclusively craftsmanship, and Stravinsky himself now denies that he ever meant to say that his music is in no sense "expressive." That his music is the product of a refined craftsmanship there can be no doubt, but that it is no more than a simple flat statement which is the mere aggregate of its parts is never true. Nor is it merely decorative or merely constructivist—any more than is the cubism of Picasso, with which it has many analogies. Just as cubism is a poetic statement about objects and forms, about the nature of vision and the way we perceive and know forms, and about the experience of art and the artistic transformation of objects and forms, so is Stravinsky's music a poetic statement about musical objects and aural forms, about the way we hear and the way we perceive and understand aural forms, about our experience of musical art and the artistic transformation of musical materials, always measured in that special domain of musical experience, time.

In 1922, Stravinsky wrote the one-act opera *Mavra*, dedicated to the memories of Glinka, Pushkin, and Tchaikovsky; six years later he wrote a ballet, *Le Baiser de la fée*, which so thoroughly absorbs and transforms music of Tchaikovsky that it is often virtually impossible to tell where Tchaikovsky leaves off and Stravinsky begins. These works, particularly the Tchaikovsky ballet, shocked those followers of Stravinsky who understood classicism as a historic and esthetic principle. In actual fact, Stravinsky can be said to have derived his neo-classical taste directly from his nineteenth-century predecessors; Tchaikovsky himself wrote a prototype of a neo-classical work in a suite based on Mozart. The very close relationship between Stravinsky's music and the nineteenth century is often overlooked. Stravinsky's real musical inheritance from the immediate past has, after the early ballets, little to do with romantic exoticism or lushness and nothing at all to do with the Wagnerian music drama and giant symphonic style; but it has a great deal to do with the *salon* and the fashionable theatre of the ballet and French-Italian opera. The *salon* and ballet traditions preserved certain classical ideas of closed form and a simple, closed melodic-harmonic style which are in fact to be found (suitably transformed, of course) in *Le Baiser de la fée*, in the Piano Sonata and *Sérénade en La*, in the *Duo Concertant* for violin and piano of 1922, in the *Four Etudes* for orchestra of 1928–1930, in the *Capriccio* for piano and orchestra of 1929, and, along with certain classical derivations, in the ballet *Apollon Musagète* of 1928. To be sure, like any musical ideas used by Stravinsky, these elements are treated in typical Stravinskyian fashion. The essence of the technique always lies, not in the source of the ideas, but in the character and technique of the transformations.

Beginning with the Piano Concerto of 1923–1924, another element enters into many of Stravinsky's works which we might characterize as a tendency (related to that of "synthetic cubism") to construct prototypical, abstracted materials and forms. This is particularly true of the whole series of symphonic and concerted works written in the 1930's and 1940's, but it is already fully developed in the big opera-oratorio based on Sophocles' *Oedipus Rex* (1927). The text, by Jean Cocteau, consists of a series of short and simple narrations in the vernacular which punctuate big arias, duets, and choruses written originally in French but translated into a solemn, dead, hierarchical and prototypical language: Latin. *Oedipus Rex* is not tragedy or even, in the ordinary sense, drama—nothing actually happens except what we are told about between the scenes—but it contains an abstracted idea of mythic-ritual musical drama refined almost down to the skeletal framework. The simplest possible diction is everywhere employed, and this laconic declamation is organized into blocked-out set–speeches and choruses. The narrator stands apart in modern clothes; the characters, although costumed and masked, have neither individuality nor the power to act—they are not even symbolic in the conventional sense but merely abstracted, particular manifestations of a human condition. There is no motion, because whatever transpires is preordained; all that is necessary is to reveal it. The motion that is lacking on the stage is offered by the music in the form of rhetorical gesture, and almost every gesture—like the myth itself—is a familiar one. The music of *Oedipus* is not really operatic or dramatic, but it represents the "idea" of those things. The very conventionality of the musical figures (Creon's trombone triad tune, the Verdiana in Jocasta's aria and the following duet with Oedipus, the grand opera music of the "Gloria," and so forth) suggests detachment, abstraction, and generalization; but these materials are also redefined through context. Context (what Stravinsky calls "manner") is everything and it is the context—the new environment—that gives the familiar and conventional gestures a new and powerful inevitability. Thus, *Oedipus* is not at all Verdian or Handelian—just as it is not really a Greek tragedy any more. It is not "about" the tragedy of a Greek hero or of anyone at all but about tragedy itself—the form and artistic experience of tragedy in its grandest operatic-oratorio guise.

In the same way, the subject matter of the Violin Concerto of 1931 is the conception of the concerto—the relationship between solo and tutti. The concerti grossi of 1938 and 1946, the important symphonies of 1940 and 1945, the trivial *Danses concertantes* of 1942 and *Scènes de ballet* of 1944, even the *Ebony Concerto* of 1945 are all in some sense archetypical. Only the theatre works of the period—the ballet *Jeu de cartes* of 1936, *Perséphone* of 1933 with its mixture of narration (text by André Gide) and dance, and the ballet *Orpheus* of 1946 with its subtle on-going baroque forms—show an independent line of thought. But the two major works of the 1940's are, in widely differing ways, again prototypical: the *Mass* for men's and boy's voices and ten instruments (1948) in its medieval evocations and the opera *The Rake's Progress* (1951) (to an ironic "classical" libretto by W. H. Auden and Chester Kallman) in its re-creation of operatic gesture, convention, and pattern. *The Rake's Progress* is a kind of meta-opera, a second-degree opera whose subject matter is largely opera itself. It is also, among other things, a compendium of Stravinskyian style and form and the last gasp of neo-classicism; with the *Cantata* of 1952 Stravinsky began again to modify his creative outlook in new directions.

It is important to realize that these "second-order" forms stand outside classical procedure, to which they are no more bound than Stravinsky's melodic ideas—even when explicitly borrowed—are committed to classical continuations. Classical forms and types are based on process; they evolve according to tonal principles and it is through this process of evolution that they come to be. Stravinsky's types are not involved with process and tonal function and come into being through statement and assertion. Classical music defines its time span through a chain of processes and developing relationships; Stravinsky organizes his time spans by precise, given articulations and rhythmic divisions. As we have said, classical form is the result of the on-going process of functional tonality; with Stravinsky, form is prior and itself creates the tonality.

Stravinsky himself has spoken of his technique of "composing by interval" and of his use of "polarity" as a tonal organizing principle. What is achieved in classical usage by a network of contrapuntal motion away from and back towards goals which are themselves defined by this motion is represented in Stravinsky by the repetition or sustaining of a single chord or harmonic pattern; by a stated, fixed set of relationships between tones which remain constant for a movement or a piece. There is nothing inevitable about the tonal centers in Stravinsky's music; they are present and effective because they are stated and asserted to be so; and the means of assertion—repetition, ostinato, pedal-points, juxtaposition of melodic and harmonic levels centering on specific tones and intervals, accent and articulation, rhythmic and metrical displacement—provide the basis for both the tonality and the form.

Most of these techniques can be observed in their highest and most effective form in the *Symphony of Psalms*, written in 1930 for the fiftieth anniversary of the Boston Symphony Orchestra. This work, for chorus and large orchestra without violins or violas, uses excerpts from the Vulgate Latin version of three Psalms; Stravinsky specifies that they must be sung in Latin. The work opens with an E–minor triad, spaced, scored, and articulated in a very characteristic manner (Example 5-1a). The short, isolated, mezzo-forte sound, which recurs half a dozen times in precisely the same form, strongly emphasizes the minor third between E and G, one of the pivotal relationships of the work. The figurations that follow are based on arpeggios and scales that refer to E–flat and C, two of the principal tonal areas of the work, themselves separated by a minor third. The piece, as it turns out, is in a kind of super C, compounded out of the related keys and triads of C minor, E–flat, E minor and, to a much more limited degree G. We might represent this tonality or polar center like this:

At the outset, however, E minor dominates, with a secondary tendency to move towards a G_7 and through a flat area. At ④ the altos enter with a "thematic" idea—nothing more than E's and F's—over a version of the arpeggio figure now slowed up to eighth notes and including a new figure based on minor thirds a half-step apart (Example 5-1b). By ⑤ the impulse has carried the music to a G area (the omnipresent thirds are D and F in the soprano voice); the figuration remains stable although expanded. This impulse is checked by the ambiguous, compound harmony and instrumental melodic figuration at [6] , and [7] is a return to point zero, but now more developed and intensified. By [9] the piece is heavily settled on the basic E and it remains so right up until the end of the movement, where the E to F melodic motion suddenly carries up to G while the bass struggles down through a B–flat and an A–flat to come to rest on its own G (Example 5-1c).

a. First movement, opening measures.

b. First movement, thematic idea.

EXAMPLE 5-1. Stravinsky, *Symphony of Psalms*. Copyright 1931 by Russischer Musikverlag; renewed 1958. Copyright and renewal assigned 1947 to Boosey & Hawkes, Inc. Revised version copyright 1948 by Boosey & Hawkes, Inc. Reprinted by permission.

c. First movement, closing measures.

d. Second movement, opening of instrumental fugue.

EXAMPLE 5-1 continued.

54

e. Second movement, opening of choral fugue.

f. Second movement, closing measures.

EXAMPLE 5-1 continued.

g. Third movement, opening measures.

h. Third movement, orchestral interlude.

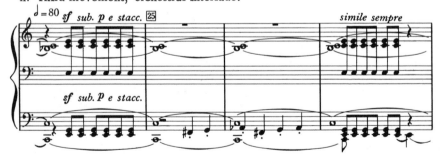

EXAMPLE 5-1 continued.

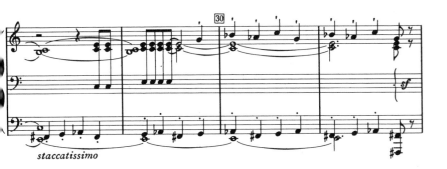

staccatissimo

i. Third movement, at 22 .

EXAMPLE 5-1 continued.

EXAMPLE 5-1 continued.

The second movement begins with a long woodwind fugue in C (minor) with a theme based on the pair of minor thirds a half-step apart already heard in the first movement (C-E-flat; B-D) (Example 5-1d). The chorus enters in E–flat minor with its own fugue subject, which is developed over the continuation of the original woodwind subject (Example 5-1e). There is a brief *a cappella* stretto, a pause, a very intense compound of the main material, and then a very quiet final few measures in which repeated choral E–flats hover over a harmonic and contrapuntal complex which ends the movement and implies the next (Example 5-1f). This opens in a modified C with a strong infusion of E–flats (and B–flats) (Example 5-1g); at the cadence, this E–flat/B–flat turns to a clear, bright C. The last time this C comes around, it does not shake off the B–flat, which remains as part of a long pedal around which appear C major punctuation in the horns (with the familiar E-G at the bottom), a little half-step plucked figure centered on G, and a melodic line rising from G through A–flat and B–flat to C (Example 5-1h). The pedal sound pushes up to D and E, the bass picks up the G to C movement, then drops through the flats back to G and down to F at a big moment of climax. The climax is built on E and A triads with a bass that centers on F and

G–sharp eventually dropping through a long chain of thirds down to C. The E-G relationship of the opening movement is echoed by a C-E–flat relationship here, while the half-step melodic figures of the opening are turned into whole steps. With the rhythmic, repeated-note "Laudate dominum" at 8 , the chorus returns to the pivotal E, and the continuation at 9 takes off from a very subtle extension of the basic E-G relationship, now clearly connected with the C major seventh chord that is so characteristic of this movement. After the opening "Alleluia" recurs, the quick tempo returns with repeated E–flats and then a modified restatement of "Laudate Dominum" on the repeated E-G minor third and later another one on a B–flat triad. At 20 , the movement and tempo settle down briefly in G over an ostinato which at first consists of a G major triad but later turns into a big trio of fourths under a simple melodic ostinato based principally on the notes E–flat-D-C at 22 (Example 5-1i). This E–flat sound is the solid and static state of the piece until the very last measures, when only the B–flat of the ostinato remains in the bass. The "Alleluia" returns—the top is suddenly discovered to come right out of the long "Laudate" that came before—and the E–flat-E–natural-G ambiguity is definitively dispelled in the final C with its E–natural on top.

Bibliography

The development and change in Stravinsky's own esthetic views over a period of years would require a text unto itself; to the sources already given at the end of Chapter 3, the important *Poetics of Music* (Cambridge, Mass., 1947) should be added. Out of the mass of Stravinskyiana, two translations might be mentioned: Heinrich Strobel's *Stravinsky: Classic Humanist* (New York, 1955), and Roman Vlad's *Stravinsky* (New York, 1960). Several collections of essays honoring Stravinsky have appeared at different periods of his life: Merle Armitage, ed., New York, 1936; Edwin Corle, ed., New York, 1949 (adopting material from the Armitage book); 75th birthday issue of *The Score*, London, May–June 1957; 80th birthday issue of *The Musical Quarterly*, New York, 1962 (also reprinted, paperback, New York, 1963). A modern analytic view of Stravinsky's musical techniques appears in Arthur Berger's "Problems of Pitch Organization in Stravinsky" (*Perspectives of New Music*, Fall–Winter, 1963, v. 2, No. 1). A recent discussion of the "neo-classical" problem appears in Edward T. Cone's "The Uses of Convention: Stravinsky and His Models" (*Musical Quarterly*, July 1962). Eric Walter White's *Stravinsky* (University of California, 1966) is a useful reference work.

6

Neo-Classicism and
Neo-Tonality in France

Classicism—defined both historically as a return to certain periods of high accomplishment and style and esthetically as the use of certain strict intellectual standards of form and form-enclosed content—has always been an important element in French culture, all the more so since French tradition itself lies somewhat outside the organic development of classical norms. Thus, the classical impulse which periodically recurs in French painting right up to Picasso has always been based on a rationalization of the external trappings of the antique as transmitted by the masters of the Italian Renaissance and early Baroque. Similarly, French musical classicism through the nineteenth and well into the twentieth century was not based on French tradition itself—French tradition is not strong on symphonic-tonal practice, and France produced little important "classical" instrumental music—but on an external, rational synthesis of the practice of the Central European masters. This kind of classicism, extensively taught at the Paris Conservatoire and constantly recurring in French music even through the crisis of Wagnerism that shook French music at the end of the nineteenth century, was by no means very deeply concerned with the fundamental techniques of classical tonality but rather with its external manifestations. Thus, paradoxically, the classical system, never deeply rooted in French musical thought, was rather easily undermined and replaced by Debussy and Stravinsky; yet, on the other hand, non-classical and neo-classical tonal practice is an essential and strong part of modern French music up until recently.[1]

Ravel

As pointed out earlier, the notion of an impressionist "school" in French music is of dubious validity. Even in his earlier and most characteristically Debussyesque works, Ravel maintains a certain independence from the complex, shifting sonorities and ambiguous tonal relationships of the older composer. Ravel was always more of a classicist than Debussy, yet paradoxically his musical thinking was always far less abstract. He was, in his way, a far more brilliant orchestrator than Debussy, yet his orchestration was imposed from the outside and was never as organic as that of Debussy. Ravel produced no independent, abstract orchestral music except for two piano concertos; virtually everything else stems from the theater or the dance, or is orchestrated from piano works. Nevertheless, the strong strain of classicism in Ravel's work is present from his earliest period; in his later years it became a dominant factor in his music. The early *Menuet* and the famous *Pavane*, the *String Quartet* of 1902–1903 and, to a lesser extent, the song cycles *Shéhérazade* (1902) and *Histoires naturelles* (1906) with their refined elegance, all show, not only classical forms, but also a notable tendency to enrich the traditional harmonic and color vocabulary while remaining close to the constraints and conditions of classical practice. The one-act comic opera, *L'Heure espagnole* (1907), uses the shifting ninth and eleventh chords, parallel structures, tonal ambiguities, and color phrases of impressionism, but even where obvious classical form is not used, the clarity of texture and line, the directionality of the musical motion, as well as the dry, detached wit (and even the use of popular,

---

[1] (This is equally true of another country in which the classical tradition was even weaker—the United States. On the one hand, this country could produce Ives and a strong avant-garde position outside the European tradition; on the other, the United States has also produced a late-blooming "neo-tonal" style in the works of Copland and others whose commitment and influence have remained strong over a period of years.)

Maurice Ravel at the seashore, Saint-Jean-de-Luz, near his native village of
Ciboure on the Basque coast of France. Sketch by Alexandre Benoit. Meyer
Collection, Paris. Reproduction forbidden.

Spanish elements) suggest the strong influence of certain aspects of classical tradition.

Most of Ravel's other pre-war works, culminating in the ballet *Daphnis et Chloé* (1909–1911), are much more clearly related to Debussy; indeed they have served as better prototypes of "impressionism" than any works of Debussy. However, even before the war (and hence even before Stravinsky), Ravel began to simplify his style in the direction of greater clarity of means and economy of expression. The *Trois Poèmes de Mallarmé* of 1913 uses voice, piano, string quartet, two flutes, and two clarinets, and the Piano Trio of 1914 shows a careful and deliberate attempt to revive old or create new "classical" forms. *Le Tombeau de Couperin*, first written for piano and later orchestrated, also dates from this period; its relationship to eighteenth-century practice is explicit.

Ravel's post-war music, beginning with *La Valse* in 1920, shows an enormous expansion of technique within the clearly formed stylistic lines of his earlier music; works like the Sonata for violin and cello of 1920–1922 and the *Chansons madécasses* for voice, piano, flute, and cello (1926) use freely dissonant harmonic and linear combinations in ways that go far beyond the old tonal and even "impressionist" techniques. The popular *Boléro* of 1928 is exceptional in Ravel's works for its intentionally primitive style, but its primitivism conceals a great deal of art; the obsession with a single idea and the assertive, unrelenting C-major tonality which breaks just before the end are as much a part of the effect as is the distinctive instrumentation. Following the charming *L'Enfant et les sortilèges* (1924; text by Colette)—virtually a "number opera" with its succession of picturesque arias and ensembles—Ravel's important late works are two piano concertos written in 1930–1931, one in D for the left hand alone, the other in G for two hands. These works, worlds away from "impressionism," represent new directions for Ravel. Both show elements of jazz and create tonal feeling by the use of added tones and appoggiatura chords; the effect of these new values that have been attached to the concepts of consonance and dissonance is somewhat analogous to that of Debussy's last sonatas, and it is exactly that achieved by certain modern jazz musicians who violate functional tonality at every chord yet in some sense also re-create it out of a new set of conventions. It is perhaps significant that, of all the major masters of the century, Ravel had the least influence on the development of contemporary ideas but possibly the greatest influence on the popular musical imagination.

"Les Six"

Ravel's neo-classicism was essentially a refinement of and a growth out of his Debussyism, modified by a refined original temperament, a taste for jazz and for Spanish music, and an ability to assimilate new ideas.

The composers of "Les Six" on the other hand were strongly anti-Debussy from the start (not to mention anti-Wagner, anti-Fauré, and anti-D'Indy as well), and they cultivated light popular, music-hall, and café style as well as jazz. There was actually never any consistent or coherent esthetic position that related the work of the six young composers, who were named as a group almost accidently, through an obvious analogy with the Russian nationalist "Five." Satie was their sponsor, and they were strongly influenced by his formidable musico-literary irreverence and irrelevance. To some extent, the literary and artistic movements of Dada and surrealism are also reflected in their music; but it is curious that the nihilist, anti-art of the Dadaists and the intense, associative and disassociative psychological techniques of the surrealists found little echo in the music of the period beyond a mild and witty use of quotation and parody.

Two of "Les Six," Louis Durey (b. 1888) and Germaine Tailleferre (b. 1892), wrote little of importance; a third, Georges Auric (b. 1899) wrote one notable ballet score and a good deal of latter-day film music. Arthur Honegger (1892–1955), a Swiss, had little relation stylistically to the rest of the group and must be considered separately. The music of "Les Six" today is represented almost entirely by the work of Darius Milhaud (b. 1892) and Francis Poulenc (1899–1963).

The creative output of Milhaud is staggering and it is almost impossible to make any effective generalizations about it. Milhaud had the most rigorous classical training at the Conservatoire; this, added to his natural proficiency, produced a composing technique of the utmost facility. In general he uses a rich harmonic vocabulary derived from pile-ups of thirds and triads combined with a very simple, flexible, melodic sense. Milhaud developed a kind of free counterpoint of triads and triad-like formations which in turn suggested a counterpoint of tonal areas. The idea of the manipulation of simultaneous tonalities—"polytonality"—already employed before World War I by Bartók (the *Bagatelles* for piano) and Charles Ives (the choral *67th Psalm*), achieved a certain importance in the 1920's. This expansion of tonal thought seemed to offer new possibilities for known materials and structures: Milhaud made a conscious attempt to create polytonal movement and form in early works such as *Les Choéphores* and *Saudades do Brasil* (1921). The notion of "polytonality" as such, however, had little further development; in a sense, the concept of different yet simultaneous tonalities is self-contradictory. The derivation and perceptibility of harmonic structures made out of interlocking or juxtaposed triads may be unquestionable, but long strings of these "poly-chords"—no matter how separated in space and timbre—cannot meaningfully establish simultaneous, contradictory tonal centers. Indeed, the significance of "polytonality" in Milhaud's music is neither formal nor systematic but is is to be found rather in the use of separate bands or layers of sound which, in works like the ballet *L'Homme et son désir*, actually form a polyphony made up of densities of sound. Often the use of diatonic ideas which clash with and contradict each other has a specifically witty intent. The forms are generally small, derived from vocal and dance patterns, and full of quotes and parodies of popular, dance, folk, jazz, café, and music-hall music. A great number of these pieces are "occasional" in nature, written with some specific purpose in mind; others seem like mere idle amusement for composer or performer. There is an off-hand quality about much of Milhaud's music that goes beyond the inevitable unevenness of a prolific composer and takes on the character of an esthetic position.

Milhaud has also written a great quantity of extended and serious instrumental work, mainly for chamber combinations, but his most important contributions have undoubtedly been in the theatre, where he has collaborated with writers of the stature of Paul Claudel, Cocteau, and Franz Werfel. Milhaud has always responded imaginatively to the theatrical situation. His "Orestes" trilogy, written with Claudel and including most notably *Les Choéphores* (1915–1916), makes notable use of a number of new and combined techniques including narration and rhythmic speaking-chorus with percussion. The ballet *L'Homme et son désir* (1918) employs instrumental forces disposed in particular spatial arrangements, a prophetic idea. The famous *Le Boeuf sur le toit* of 1919 is a compendium of popular tunes, mostly South American in origin (Milhaud had been an attaché in the French embassy at Rio de Janeiro during World War I), and treated in a noisy, rattling, racy manner. *La Création du monde*, a ballet of 1923, often considered Milhaud's masterpiece, is the first major composition to make extensive, serious, and subtle use of jazz. Milhaud did not actually "write" jazz, but the music is imbued with the sound and style of the jazz of that day.

The list could be extended. *Le Pauvre Matelot* of 1916 is a curiously grim but effective piece of verismo opera with a text by Cocteau. At another extreme are the infinitesimal *"opéras minutes"* of the following year with their absurdly condensed bits of classical tragedy. And the *Christophe Colomb of* 1929–30 presents still another huge contrast; it is a very grand symbolic opera with an allegorical text by Claudel and a musical and dramatic apparatus of considerable weight and power.

The pairing of Milhaud with his contemporary Francis Poulenc has obvious historical and even some esthetic justification, but they are in fact two vastly different musical personalities. Milhaud, the intensely trained "natural" musician, was brought up in the classical tradition and rejected it or used it to his own ends with the utter ease of a fluent and prolific master. Poulenc, virtually self-taught, slowly and painstakingly re-created tradition in a series of small, witty, elegant, and fastidious pieces, carefully worked out almost from note to note. This, of course, is not the Poulenc of wide popularity, composer of *buffa* works like *Le Bal masqué* (1932), the *Concerto for Two Pianos* (1932), and *Les Mamelles de Tirésias* (1944) where wrong notes, movie music, barroom ballads, and sentimental chansons jostle each other in racy profusion. It is rather the Poulenc who was a direct heir to the nineteenth-century neo-classical and salon tradition—a durable factor in French musical life. A work like the Organ Concerto (1938), although superficially derived from Bach, is really a direct descendant of the lyric, popular classicism of composers like Viotti and Saint-Saëns. Traces of this lyric gift are actually present even in the most outrageous of the parody-and-quote pieces, and a simple, *cantabile* expression can be found in much of the piano and a good deal of the chamber music. It was present already in early works like the ballet *Les Biches* (1923); it is the dominant musical speech in the simple, effective *Dialogues des Carmélites* (1957), which crosses Duparc with Mussorgsky, and in choral works like *Stabat Mater* (1951), *Gloria* (1960), and the *Sept Répons du Ténèbre* (1962). But Poulenc's gift for lyric line is most evident in his songs, among which are his most attractive and successful works, and which, apart from the very different case of Strauss, represent a clearer continuation or reinstatement of the tradition than any other works we shall be discussing in this book.

The third important member of "Les Six" scarcely belongs with the others at all; Honegger's connection with "Les Six" really came about through his association with his fellow-pupil Milhaud and through the intellectual and moral patronage of Satie. Honegger's starting point was the Central European tradition up to and including even early Schoenberg but tempered considerably by Debussy and the Russians. His first reputation was based on a semi-dramatic biblical oratorio, *Le Roi David* (1921), and on several picturesque orchestral works: *Pastorale d'été* (1921), *Pacific 231* (the famous musical railroad train of 1924), and *Rugby* (1928). His reputation as the composer of picturesque, noisy, avant-garde tone poems is, however, misleading. *Le Roi David*, originally conceived, like *L'Histoire du soldat*, as a stage work with spoken narration and dialogue, mime, and dance, was scored for a chamber ensemble and intentionally built around a simple, almost popular melodic style. Even in the later concert version for large orchestra, the essentially simple closed forms remain unaltered, and the modified, unsystematic modal tonality remains fundamental to the effect; only the big contrapuntal choruses that close the main sections of the piece have extended classical form. Honegger returned to this genre in 1938 with the popular *Jeanne d'Arc au bûcher;* and *Le Roi David* itself is the prototype for a widespread popular choral style built on simple modal tonality, modest choral counterpoint, local color, and small, easily apprehended forms. Honegger himself was concerned with the expansion of these techniques (minus the pseudo-Orientalisms of *Le Roi David*) into a more complex contrapuntal symphonic and chamber style: in the list of his later works, large-scale symphonic and chamber works predominate. Long lines, moving across large, free diatonic and modal areas, with harmonic structures built on accumulations of thirds and added diatonic tones, and a highly accented but basically regular, even motoric rhythmic structure are the hallmarks of a style that accommodated the classical tradition to a modified, conservative, and accessible twentieth-century style of considerable flexibility and, in the hands of a Honegger at least, a good deal of expressive effect. Like the much more consistent and highly organized tonal style developed by Hindemith in his later years, the idiom had considerable influence over a period of about a quarter of a century. Honegger's work represented a strong and serious recasting of tradition in a style that had, in spite of serious formal defects (structures far too extended for the light tonal supports), a certain amount of scope and purpose; as such it remained one of the starting points for twentieth-century tonal symphonic tradition.

Bibliography

In addition to the Ravel book noted at the end of Chapter 3, mention might be made of a view from the avant-garde: Pierre Boulez's "Trajectoires: Ravel, Stravinsky, Schoenberg" in vol. 6 of *Contrepoints* (Paris, 1949). Material on "Les Six" includes Henri Hell's *Poulenc* (New York, 1959), Darius Milhaud's autobiographical *Notes Without Music* (New York, 1953), and, in French, Honegger's *Je suis compositeur* (Paris, 1951).

7
Neo-Classicism and Neo-Tonality Outside of France

Hindemith and Gebrauchsmusik

The most systematic of the new tonal styles was that developed by Paul Hindemith (1895–1963). Hindemith was the youngest of the first group of major twentieth-century pioneers, and his artistic development follows the general pattern of the early decades but at a distance of some years. Thus his early work, written at about the time of World War I and shortly thereafter, comes out of the Central European line—the tradition of Brahms and Max Reger, however, rather than that of Wagner. Like Reger, Hindemith extended the chromatic range with great mastery, always in terms of the great contrapuntal tradition; to the end of his life, Hindemith remained a contrapuntist. With the early string sonatas of 1920–1923 (Opus 11), we are already in the composer's first mature phase.

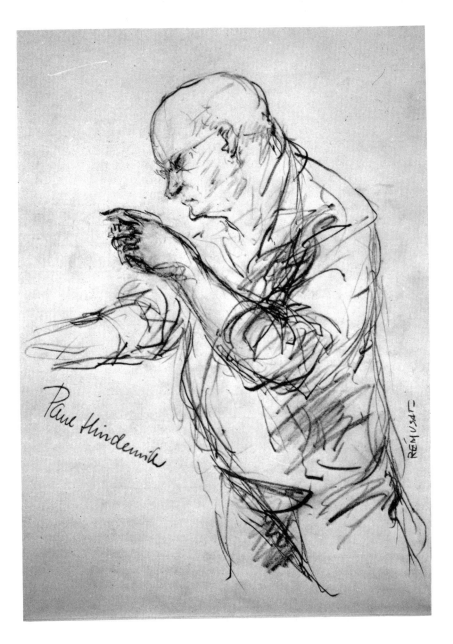

Paul Hindemith by Rémusat. Meyer Collection, Paris. Reproduction forbidden.

A long series of important works followed: the one-act operas of 1921, *Cardillac* of 1925, *Hin und Zurück* and *Neues vom Tage* of 1927 and 1929, the song cycles *Die junge Magd* and *Das Marienleben* of 1922 and 1924, more sonatas for strings, a series of string quartets, a number of works for piano, the famous *Kleine Kammermusik* for winds (Op. 24, No. 2) of 1922, and a group of concerted works with chamber orchestra. All of this music had a contrapuntal aggressiveness and a free use of dissonance that led to its being described as "atonal"; it now seems neither systematically tonal nor really atonal. The harmonic sense and the big construction of the lines, though often extremely chromatic, nearly always suggest a clear but undefined sense of underlying tonal shape and direction, while a rather intense, expressive invention dominates the surface. Works like *Das Marienleben* (in its original version) come very close in many ways to the style of the Viennese expressionists; on the other hand, pieces like the piano suite *1922* and some of the *Kammermusik* compositions show a wit and an irreverent boisterousness that approach and even —in matters of satire and irony—outdo "Les Six."

About 1927, Hindemith began to change his musical style and outlook a good deal in the direction of simplicity and clarity, and towards a careful new tonal style which was to characterize his music until his death. In the end, Hindemith's style was conditioned by a number of factors, nearly all of which derived from his extraordinary musicality. Hindemith was an exceptional type of "natural" musician; he composed with extraordinary facility and he was the only important composer of the first part of the century who was also an important performing artist and conductor. Almost all of Hindemith's works of the 1920's (including the operas) were conceived for chamber performance, often with the composer himself playing the violin, viola, or viola d'amore; and he was one of the first modern musicians to explore—through performance as well as research—the vast areas of early music. He was a well-known teacher and an influential theorist. In 1927 Hindemith formulated a definitive statement of his conception of the role of the composer in society; like Stravinsky, he placed great emphasis on the composer as craftsman, but he also stressed the importance of the relationship between the composer and the performer. In the late 1920's and early 1930's he wrote a series of ensemble and solo works for amateur and student performance, including a musical play for children and a whole day's worth of music written for young students at a school. On a more advanced level came a long series of sonatas for virtually every important instrument and a further series of concerted works for solo instruments with small and large orchestras. This so-called *Gebrauchsmusik* or "music for use" represents in part a return—or at least an idealization—of the old relationships that had existed between composers, performers, patrons, and audiences before the nineteenth century. The romantic composer was presumably inspired by an inner compulsion, by a need to communicate something; Hindemith was inspired by a commission, by the presence of a performer (himself perhaps), and by the reality of an actual performing situation. It is probable that the reestablishment of the composer-performer relationship, and of the significance of the realities of performance and the performance situation, was Hindemith's most enduring theoretical contribution.

As a theorist, however, Hindemith wanted to accomplish a great deal more than that. Coincident with the establishment of the *Gebrauchsmusik* ideal came the simplification of his style and the definitive return to tonal ways of thinking. This is clear, not only in the solo and chamber works, but also in the major compositions of the 1930's and 1940's, beginning with the *Konzertmusik* for strings and brass of 1930 and continuing with the opera *Mathis der Maler* (1934), the symphony extracted from it, a pair of concertos for orchestra, and several ballet scores. During this period Hindemith also began to systematize his ideas in a fashion which ultimately resulted in a series of theoretical works (never completed) and in the big, didactic cycle of fugues and interludes for piano published in 1943 as *Ludus Tonalis*. Hindemith consciously attempted to formulate a new tonal system which, growing out of certain acoustical principles and some fundamental notions of linear counterpoint, was to include a complete range of chromatic expression. The basic conception was that of the weight and tension of individual intervals, determined by an acoustic and psychological classification and revealed through a system of harmonic and melodic necessity (derived in part from the overtone series). Hindemith's music after the late 1920's was increasingly based on such ideas. Tonal centers are established by a kind of gravitational melodic movement and a harmonic motion based on chords of greater and lesser tension; the triad remains primary, the focal point of cadence and rest.[1] This remarkable parallel to the old tonal system—based, not on tradition and usage, but on presumed acoustical and psychological validities—was adopted by the composer himself in such a thorough-going manner that he even returned to some of his important older works and revised them in order to make them conform more closely to his later thinking—e.g. *Das Marienleben*, revised in 1948 (see example 7-1).

Although Hindemith thought of his theoretical ideas and method of teaching as a synthesis, they have in fact proved to be relevant only to certain kinds of music—principally Hindemith's own. For Hindemith himself, however (less so perhaps for his pupils and imitators), they provided a way of achieving a coherent kind of musical speech which could sustain invention and produce consistent and large-scale forms in an individual and contemporary kind of tonal language. Hindemith's later works fit the patterns thus established—his opera based on the life of Kepler, *Die Harmonie der Welt* (1956); his opera based on Thornton Wilder's *The*

---

[1] Hindemith's classification of chordal structures, of intervals, and of triadic relationships has been described as a tonal system without the notion of "Key." The classical system would then be, presumably, a special case of this wider theoretical principle.

a. Comparison of opening measures.

EXAMPLE 7-1. Hindemith, *Das Marienleben*, "*O hast du dies gewollt*"; 1922–1923 and 1948 versions. Quoted by permission of B. Schott's Söhne, Mainz.

b. Comparison of closing measures.

EXAMPLE 7-1 continued.

Long Christmas Dinner (1960); the Whitman setting *When Lilacs Last in the Dooryard Bloom'd* (1946); the *Octet* (1956); and the later choral works. Hindemith tried to synthesize the great linear tradition with a kind of chromatically accented tonality; in doing so he created an individual style with its unmistakable sound of major and minor seconds, fourths and fifths. Everything moves, everything works, everything is under perfect control; the music lies well for the instruments, and within its narrow rhythmic compass, it swings along. Hindemith can be expressive; he is always idiomatic, sometimes routine. He himself considered his later work as a logical and maturing development out of his wilder young days; but probably his major creative power was put into those early unfettered works, and certainly, the early versions of the revised works are preferable.

There is unquestionably a logic and—up to a point at least—an inner development in Hindemith's work. Unlike other prolific composers, Hindemith was never uncritical about his own work; his standards of craftsmanship never flagged, only his inspiration. When his imagination was equal to his craft—the standard of invention is especially high in his dramatic works—he was able to turn his personal synthesis of theory and practice into the highest artistic communication.

The diffusion of neo-classicism

Neo-classicism or neo-tonality in one form or another became the dominant international idea in the 1930's and 1940's. It has been said, with a great deal of truth, that neo-classicism as such hardly constitutes a "style" or a "school," and indeed the broadest impact of the new tonal techniques was on the development of the new national styles to be discussed in the next chapter. There remain, however, a number of composers and works to be mentioned here whose outlook, essentially international in character, was strongly conditioned by classic ideals as interpreted through new tonal forms.

In France, there are several lesser figures who, while officially outside of "Les Six," were related to them in style and temperament. The most important of these are Jacques Ibert (1890–1962) and Jean Françaix (b. 1912), two witty, minor talents whose esthetic ranges from a kind of neo-impressionism (Ibert's *Escales* of 1922) to a musical jollity that is very close to Poulenc and Milhaud (Ibert's wind quintet; Françaix's concertino for piano and orchestra). Mention should also be made here of the later work of Vincent d'Indy (1851–1931). D'Indy, who derived from Franck, was an important pedagogue, and the Schola Cantorum, of which he was director from its inception in 1900 to his death, was an important center of new ideas as well as of the revival of old ones. Under d'Indy's direction, the Schola pioneered in the modern and authentic performance of old music; it also evolved new techniques of teaching composition. D'Indy's own work is a curious mixture of a rich Franck-Wagner late-nineteenth-century symphonic style, a sense of classical technique and form, an expanded modern chromatic palette somewhat cautiously used, and a love of folk song and folk-song-like simplicity. Some of these ideas were carried further by d'Indy's pupil Albert Roussel (1869–1937) who, starting with a kind of amalgamation of d'Indy and Debussy, achieved an individual neo-classical style whose development seems parallel to rather than directly influenced by the work of a composer like Stravinsky.

The classical tradition was, in great part, Italian, but neo-classicism as an intellectual or expressive idea has had a relatively minor role in modern Italian musical life, with one major exception. Alfredo Casella (1883–1947), a once influential, now neglected composer, developed a tonal style based on a free use of the seven diatonic steps combined with strong classical forms derived from the Monteverdi-Scarlatti tradition. Casella was an important figure in Italian musical life and he played a major role in the revival of Italian instrumental music; he also helped to create a modern Italian tonal idiom and to insure that ultra-chromatic, atonal, and twelve-tone ideas would not penetrate Italian musical life—as, indeed, they did not until after his death. The most important younger Italian neo-classicist was Goffredo Petrassi (b. 1904) who, until his involvement in avant-gardism in the last few years, wrote a series of works in a serious, colorful, abstract, limber tonal style.[2]

In most of Europe, "neo-classicism" was long considered by many as a form of musical intellectualizing and even ultra-modernity. In Germany, however, a number of composers picked up some of the simpler aspects and techniques of Stravinsky, Hindemith, and the French to synthesize an accessible, popular, neo-tonal style. The most important of these is Carl Orff (b. 1895), whose blocky, triadic theater music is built on obsessively repeated harmonic structures, semi-chanted, repetitious melodic figurations, and a simple colorful orchestration based on percussion sounds, most of it quite clearly derived from Stravinsky, especially from *Les Noces*. Orff has applied some of these materials to a kind of creative-play teaching method for children which has had a great deal of success in Germany and elsewhere. Werner Egk (b. 1901), whose name and music are often linked with that of Orff, writes a more elaborate kind of piece, based on popular types and influenced by French style. Egk's music has simple direction and development; Orff's intentionally has none. Indeed, Orff's music stands as virtually the last and simplest representative of the esthetic of simplicity which had considerable influence in European and American music between the wars.

In the *Classical Symphony* and in many of his later works as well, Sergei Prokofiev achieved something of a tonal synthesis which constitutes an authentic and—by and large—convincing "neo-classicism"; the same is true (but to a much lesser degree) of the work of Dmitri Shostakovitch (b. 1906). In England, a work like William Walton's *Façade* is very close in wit and intent to the French style of the period, especially in its original form with Edith Sitwell's poetry recited to a chamber accompaniment. All of Benjamin Britten's highly original tonal music could be placed here; and important American works like the early music of Roger Sessions, the *Short Symphony* and other pieces of Aaron Copland, the Gertrude Stein settings of Virgil Thomson, earlier works of Elliott Carter, Lukas Foss, and

---

[2] The work of other "neo-tonal" Italians—Respighi, Pizzetti, Malipiero—is considered in Chapter 8.

Arthur Berger, most of the music of Irving Fine, many compositions by Walter Piston and Roy Harris, as well as a large group of works by younger composers show a strong neo-classical or neo-tonal bent of one kind or another. Neo-classicism was, not very long ago, an issue; it is one no longer and, as the techniques of twentieth-century tonality are assimilated or—as is now more generally the case—superseded, the old terminology seems less and less meaningful. "Neo-classicism" petered out in a series of modest styles, eclectic in nature and severely limited in scope. Composers like Stravinsky and Hindemith could re-create tonal forms out of which big pieces could be made, works which were at once clever, craftsmanlike, clear and even accessible, idiomatic and full of vitality, allied with tradition but essentially new and capable of assimilating with ease such divergent elements as quotes from the classics, folk music, jazz, parody, wit and elegance, and a great deal of serious intellectual thought and communication about the nature of musical form, craft, art, and experience. The experience was, after a certain point, too limiting, too restricted for another generation—indeed, even for Stravinsky himself. If tonality is to retain vitality, it is clear that it must find new forms.

Bibliography

There is little or no general literature on "neo-classicism," a fact which may be partly due to the inadequacy of that useful but misleading catch-all. For Hindemith, the composer's own *Craft of Musical Composition* (New York, 1941, 1942) and *A Composer's World* (Cambridge, 1952) are fundamental. A good general book in German is Heinrich Strobel's *Paul Hindemith* (Mainz, Germany, 1948). Allen Forte's *Contemporary Tone Structures* (Teachers' College, New York, 1955) is a rare and serious attempt to discuss new tonal ideas.

8

National Styles

The development of national styles outside of Central Europe and the general international evolution of twentieth-century music are closely related. The discovery of folk music, particularly that of Eastern Europe, was one of the factors that broadened the horizons of Western music. At the same time, no extensive independent developments of great significance could take place until the long dominance of the central, "common practice" tonal system was ended. In general, some new kind of tonal framework was needed within which distinctly national idioms—derived from the small forms of folk and dance music—could be expanded into larger means of creative communication. Thus, outside of Germany and France, a whole series of local styles developed, adapting influences first from Debussy and Ravel, later from Stravinsky, Hindemith, and others, to local modes of speech. In spite of the fact that the principal ideological opposition of the first part of the twentieth century was between Stravinskyian "neo-classicism" and Schoenbergian chromatic and twelve-tone ideas, it was rather the strong local and national styles which proved the principal bulwark against atonal and twelve-tone ideas. This was by no means merely a question of conservatism or of local pride. Amid the economic, political, and social crises of the late 1920's and 1930's, a dominant strain of social and esthetic thought appeared which rejected the atonal and experimental avant-gardism of the earlier part of the century in favor of a kind of musical populism, of simplicity and accessibility expressed through the use of tonal forms and of popular and folk materials.

Eastern Europe: Bartók

The most important figure to come out of Eastern Europe was Béla Bartók (1881–1945). Hungary, although an intensely musical country, had long been under the political and artistic hegemony of Vienna and Central Europe; Bartók was thoroughly trained in the traditional manner, and his early works are strongly resonant of Brahms and Richard Strauss. The liberating influences were Debussy and Magyar folk song. With Zoltán Kodály, Bartók went out into the Hungarian countryside and made the first definitive collections of Eastern European folk music. He transcribed this music in a manner virtually free of the nineteenth-century prejudices which had squeezed the highly distinctive character of folk art into the Procrustean bed of traditional tonality and which had confused genuine Hungarian folk expression with the popularized "Gypsy" music of the cafés. Bartók was not only able to establish the distinctive character of the true Magyar style; he was also able to record and distinguish other Eastern folk music of differing and equally distinct character. None of this music responds to the conventions of Central European tonal thinking. Much of it is heterophonic in nature; a drone or rhythmic accompaniment underlays a single-line melody which however appears in different versions, sometimes simultaneous and often highly embellished.

In Bartók's earliest published works, his *Rhapsody*, Op. 1 (1904) and his *Suites* for orchestra, Op. 3 and 4, (1905, 1907) the setting of the Hungarian material already owes something to Debussy; even when Bartók threw off the direct Debussy influence, a certain special kind of impressionist color and form can be found in works like *Bluebeard's Castle* (1911) and the many characteristic "Night Music" movements of the later instrumental works. In his *Two Portraits* of 1907 and, especially, in his *Bagatelles* for piano of 1908, Bartók moved quickly and with assurance into a mature and original phase—a phase quite equal and parallel to other developments elsewhere. The *Bagatelles*, besides being technical studies in new

Béla Bartók, drawn in 1944, one year before his death, by Alexander Dolbin. Meyer Collection, Paris. Reproduction forbidden.

rhythmic, melodic, and harmonic devices, also suggest the way in which Bartók stylized melodic and rhythmic ideas and extracted from them their characteristic sound qualities, now transformed into harmonies, counter-lines, and colors. In his String Quartet No. 1, also of 1908, Bartók reverts to a big contrapuntal, Central European style with a wandering kind of tonal chromaticism which is not always persuasive. But in the piano music of 1909–11—especially the well-known *Allegro barbaro*—in the *Two Pictures* for orchestra of 1910, in the two big theater works of 1911 and 1915, *Bluebeard's Castle* and the ballet *The Wooden Prince*, and in the Piano Suite, Op. 14, of 1916, Bartók develops a broad and colorful speech of great force and vitality. There is little if any actual folk material in the music, but the Hungarian character is omnipresent. The harmonic structure is still basically triadic; or, at least, the triad represents the main point of departure and return. The basic structures are tonal although, of course, not in the old sense. Bartók's tonal writing and his structural sense are not completely consistent; rather he proceeds from point to point with the modal character of the melodic invention sustained by rhythmic vitality, changing meters, Debussyian color, and parallel harmonic motion. Softer ninth- and eleventh-chord sounds, punctuated by sharp harmonic dissonance, open out at key points of articulation into triads.

At about this time Bartók must have become acquainted with recent developments in Vienna and Paris: his String Quartet No. 2 of 1917 and *The Miraculous Mandarin*, a ballet of 1919, show, respectively, strong influences from Schoenberg and Stravinsky. These two impressive works present a remarkable contrast: the former contrapuntal, highly developed, and intensely expressive in an introspective way; the latter big and violent in the manner of the sophisticated primitivism of *Le Sacre du Printemps*. It is almost as if Bartók had to recapitulate for himself the revolutionary experiences of a few years earlier in order to gain mastery of the rhythmic freedom, harmonic dissonance, color range, block-form, and additive structures of a Stravinsky and the intense, crowded, contrapuntal, expressive chromaticism and organizational control of a Schoenberg. Afterwards, Bartók was able to create his own imaginative world in which all these techniques and materials—folk-song, tonal harmonies built in thirds, ultra-chromaticism and dissonant "atonality," contrapuntal, serial construction, percussive color-rhythm—could function (often side by side) as expressive and structural ideas compatible with the special qualities of his own invention.

The 1920's were a decade of chamber composition for Bartók: the "difficult" violin and piano sonatas of 1921–1922, the Piano Sonata and *Out of Doors* suite of 1926 and the Third and Fourth String Quartets of 1927–1928 are works of great intensity in which Bartók for the first time extends his own personal style into utterances of considerable size and shape. (The construction of the theatre works, although extended, had been essentially an accumulation of localized events.) The String Quartet No. 3, with its extended one-movement construction, and No. 4, with its tightly organized transformations and returns, sustain unified lines of thought over long expressive periods through a rather subtle manipulation of a material that is imaginative in shape, limited in content, but of broad and striking implications. Thus, the half and whole steps of the opening of the Fourth Quartet, with their closely intertwined melodic and harmonic character filling out specific segments of the chromatic space (it is almost impossible to tell where harmony leaves off and "melody" begins), not only imbue the entire work with their characteristic sound but ultimately shape the entire harmonic and melodic invention (Example 8-1).

a. First movement, opening measures.

EXAMPLE 8-1. Bartók, *String Quartet No. 4*, First Movement. Copyright 1929 by Universal Edition; renewed 1956. Copyright and renewal assigned to Boosey & Hawkes, Inc. for the U.S.A. Reprinted by permission of Boosey & Hawkes, Inc. and Universal Edition.

b. First movement, closing measures.

EXAMPLE 8-1 continued.

These chamber works are built on a rhythmic and phrase character that is often strongly suggestive of folk ideas and dependent on a kind of assertive tonality-in-the-small, but they are organized in their big structure according to other principles. The typical method is one of permeating entire movements with a particular kind of sound (characteristic harmonic, melodic, and rhythmic shapes, timbres, and articulations, etc.), a method that is about midway between certain tonal techniques of Stravinsky and the more highly ordered serial construction of Schoenberg.

By contrast, Bartók's relatively few orchestral works of this period—orchestrations of folk song sets originally written for piano, the *Dance Suite* of 1923, the Piano Concerto No. 1 of 1926, and the two *Rhapsodies* for violin and orchestra of 1928—are written in a more accessible tonal vein, and the use of Hungarian material is broader and more popular in nature. Beginning with the *Cantata Profana* of 1930 and the Piano Concerto No. 2 of the following year, Bartók showed a strong tendency to synthesize these aspects of his work. Thus, although the Fifth String Quartet of 1934 is a piece of dissonant, lean and rhythmic, hard-driving Bartókiana, its tonal construction is clearer than that of the Third and Fourth; the Sixth Quartet of 1939 is built on a clear triadic tonality derived from contrapuntal movement and the juxtaposition and relationships of basic intervallic ideas built on thirds and fifths. In sound, the Sixth Quartet seems to be a reversion to an earlier, clearer tonal idiom, but in fact, the technique is an extension of ideas that appear in all of Bartók's work. Thus, Bartók's favorite cyclical treatment appears here in the form of an introduction to the various movements which constantly expands until it becomes the entire final movement; similarly, the triadic construction, although clearly tonal in nature, is also an extension of the intervallic principle which, in the earlier quartets, had been worked out of intervals like minor seconds and major sevenths replaced here by thirds and fifths.

The entire range of Bartókian techniques can be found in miniature in the remarkable series of studies which constitute his *Mikrokosmos* (1926–1937), a "Gradus ad Parnassum" not only for the piano student but also for the student of creative ideas. Most of Bartók's later works show some kind of synthesis of this very wide-ranging material combined with the broadest kind of structural methods: the *Divertimento* for strings (1939), *Music for String Instruments, Percussion, and Celesta* (1936), the *Sonata for Two Pianos and Percussion* (1937), the *Violin Concerto* (1938), *Contrasts* for clarinet, violin, and piano (1938), the *Concerto for Orchestra* (1944), the *Third Piano Concerto* (1945), and the *Viola Concerto*, finished after Bartók's death in 1945 by Tibor Serly, are compositions of a clear and open character in which tonal forms re-establish themselves in a larger context of expressive freedom. The *Music for Strings, Percussion, and Celesta*, which has perhaps the widest range of character and invention of any single work of Bartók, begins with a rather dense chromatic fugue built on one of Bartók's most characteristic melodic types: a succession of ascending and descending half and whole steps contained within a very small compass (Example 8-2a). Locally, this music does not sound tonal at all, but its broad structure which departs from and closes finally on A through harmonic and melodic cycles of fifths suggests a chromatic interpretation of long-range tonal organization. The second movement, with its rhythmic vitality enhanced by the antiphonal intertwining sound of two small ensembles, moves away from and back to a very stable tonal sound. The third movement, a characteristic piece of "Night Music," is built on isolated timbres and simple, repeated structures which dissolve into agitated motion and then re-form themselves. The big A-major finale with its folkish sound is a little incoherent by itself but it rounds off the entire work with its notable technique of reinterpreting the earlier chromatic sounds and types in diatonic and triadic-tonal terms (Example 8-2b-e).

a. First-movement theme.

EXAMPLE 8-2. Bartók, *Music for Strings, Percussion, and Celesta.* Copyright 1937 by Universal Edition; renewed 1964. Copyright and renewal assigned to Boosey & Hawkes, Inc. for the U.S.A. Reprinted by permission.

b. Chromatic material in last movement.

c. Diatonic expansion (last movement).

d. Development of diatonic figures.

e. Main theme of last movement.

Bartók's style, which for a brief time was extremely influential among younger composers, has proved too limiting and perhaps too specifically Hungarian to maintain a direct and continuous impact on the course of creative development, but the nature of his synthesis and the inclusive nature of his composing technique are perhaps of greater importance than has yet been recognized. There are universal qualities in Bartók's work which transcend the appealing and personal but perhaps limited and inconsistent surface character of the sound of his music.

Eastern Europe: Hungary and Czechoslovakia

The most important twentieth-century Hungarian composer after Bartók is Zoltán Kodály (b. 1882), Bartók's close colleague and collaborator in the great work of collecting Hungarian folk music. Kodály's best-known music is the suite derived from his musical play *Háry János*, but its rather amusing if somewhat trivial adaptations of popular and folk styles are not necessarily representative of Kodály's serious work. Kodály's music is, however, more tonally and triadically oriented than Bartók's—though not in the sense of a traditionalist like their Hungarian colleague, Ernst von Dohnányi (1877–1960). Kodály's output includes a considerable body of chamber music; especially notable are a sonata for solo cello (1915), a *Serenade* for two violins and viola (1919–1920), and two string quartets (1908, 1916–1917) which, while without Bartók's special qualities of intensity, originality, and reflective thought, are strong, lyric essays of convincing shape. Kodály's style, with its open, triadic sound and its derivation from a lyric, Hungarian melos, is eminently suited to—even derived from—the human voice. Kodály established in Hungary the principle that singing should be the basis of music education and he introduced a series of reforms and innovations in the organization and teaching of sight-singing which have had a wide influence. He wanted every child to participate in choral singing, and a great many of his own choral works are intended for performance by children, amateurs, and students. The core of Kodály's art is to be found in his songs, his choruses, and in big chorus-and-orchestra compositions like his *Psalmus Hungaricus* (1923).

A striking example of the liberation of the creative imagination of an Eastern European composer through the assimilation of new ideas is provided by the Czech composer, Leoš Janáček. Janáček, who was born in 1854 and died in 1928, was ten years older than Strauss and hardly more than a decade younger than Dvořák; for years he was a provincial music teacher in a little-known corner of what was to become Czechoslovakia, and his music was that of a provincial Dvořák. Suddenly, just at the turn of the century, his style and his creative powers broadened with the remarkable opera *Jenufa* (1904). Even so, it was more than ten years before *Jenufa* was produced in Prague and Vienna (in 1916), and it was only in the last years of his life that Janáček produced the remarkable series of original and powerful works on which his reputation now rests: *The Diary of One Who Vanished* (1916), *Katya Kabanová* (from Ostrovsky; 1919–1921), *The Cunning Little Vixen* (1921–1923), *The Makropulos Affair* (text by Capek; 1923–1924), *From the House of the Dead* (after Dostoyevsky; 1928), the *Slavonic Mass*, the *Sinfonietta* of 1926, and several chamber works. Like Kodály, Janáček combined a folk melos with a basically triadic style, but the character of Janáček's music is utterly unlike that of his younger contemporaries in Hungary—and not only because of the differences between Czech and Hungarian folk music. Janáček never used specifically folk material, but he derived his melodic speech from the prose-poetry character of Slavic folk music with its characteristic intervals and scales, its close identification with language, and the insistent, repeated character of its melodic lines. An almost obsessive concern with repetition is very characteristic, with small figures of an insistent, even prosaic character, repeated over and over in block-like sections; the larger sections are built up through the juxtaposition and contrast of these very grand and simple building-blocks arranged in strong and persistent rhythmic layers. The technique is at work in the single successful large symphonic piece—the *Sinfonietta*—but it is most basic to Janáček's dramatic works; he was, above all, a man of the theatre with an intense, intuitive understanding of the role of simplicity and the impact of repetition and striking contrast in dramatic construction. The ironic pessimism of these works—strongly in the Slavic tradition—is expressed through the rather affirmative and sophisticated naïveté of the music, and this itself produces some of the great dramatic tensions. Janáček's mature style was almost certainly achieved through his contact with the main currents of Western musical thought after World War I—Stravinsky may have been an influence—but these currents (not easily recognizable at all except in the character of lean, even angular, poetic simplicity on the surface and the "additive" construction underneath) are transformed into a style of expressive precision and dramatic originality.

Dvořák's principal pupil and successor, Josef Suk (1874–1935), began as a kind of polyphonic Dvořák whose harmonic horizons later expanded to include a range of modern techniques. In turn, Suk's best-known pupil was Bohuslav Martinu (1890–1959) who studied also with Roussel in Paris and mixed the Czech tradition with strong doses of French style (Ravel, d'Indy, Roussel), eventually turning to a rather international manner with a strong tonal and neo-classic bent.

Eastern Europe: Russia

Strong currents of ultra-traditional conservatism and radical innovation existed together in Russia from the late nineteenth century up until the Stalinist anti-modern campaigns of the 1930's. The older Romantic tradition can be represented by Sergei Rachmaninoff (1873–1943) who, although he left Russia permanently in 1917 and lived until 1943, had already composed all but two or three of his best-known works before World War I. On the other hand, the strong personality of Scriabin attracted the attention of mystically inclined younger Russian musicians, who also began to show remarkable tendencies to strike out on their own. It is difficult to say what exactly are the sources of Prokofiev's early music—partly Scriabin, perhaps, but in any event not Stravinsky. Prokofiev composed his First Piano Concerto in 1911, his early piano works between 1908 and 1913, and his First Violin Concerto in 1915–1917, before he could have known much about Stravinsky's development; and even the *Scythian Suite* of 1914, for all its obvious Stravinskyisms, is really a parallel to *Le Sacre* rather than a clear derivation from it. The *Scythian Suite* marks the beginning of a distinct period in Prokofiev's life, a development only briefly interrupted by the composer's lively reinterpretation of tradition in his *Classical Symphony*. Such works as *Sarcasms* and *Visions fugitives* for piano, the Third and Fourth Piano Sonatas, the ballet

Chout, and the opera *The Gambler* (1915–1917; after Dostoyevsky), *Sept, ils sont sept* for tenor, chorus, and orchestra—all dating from before 1920—are built on highly dissonant textures often coupled with great motoric drive. Prokofiev's music at this period had the widest range of means, and within a few years between 1919 and 1923 he produced the masterpieces of his early period, *The Love for Three Oranges* and *The Flaming Angel,* utterly contrasting works, the former satirical and ironic, written with great wit and flair, the latter intensely dramatic, expressionistic, a curious and effective combination of the ironic and the visionary.

Prokofiev, who had left Russia in 1918, went first to the United States and later to Paris where he worked throughout the 1920's, composing two ballets for Diaghilev (*Le Pas d'acier* and *L'Enfant prodigue*), his symphonies Nos. 2, 3, and 4, and his piano concertos Nos. 3, 4, and 5. After *The Flaming Angel* and the remarkable Symphony derived from it (No. 3), the music of Prokofiev's Paris period is brilliant, hard-driving, and powerful but, with one or two exceptions, not on a level with his earlier works. It is possible that he found it difficult to work in Paris and away from Russia; at any rate, in 1934 he went back and almost immediately plunged into a whole series of "practical" projects which included the scores for the films *Lieutenant Kije* and Eisenstein's *Alexander Nevsky,* the ballets *Romeo and Juliet* and *Cinderella,* the propaganda operas *Simeon Kotko* and *A Tale of a Real Man,* an operatic setting of Tolstoy's *War and Peace,* the admirable children's tale *Peter and the Wolf,* and cantatas and other vocal works with patriotic or propagandistic texts. Several chamber works, his Sixth, Seventh, and Eighth Piano Sonatas, his Violin Concerto No. 2, and his last three symphonies (including the popular Fifth) are also products of his Soviet period. Most of this music is characterized by a drastic simplification of style and, in line with the political pressures of Soviet life and some of the prevailing esthetic ideas of the period, a strong revival of tonal procedures. This stylistic evolution took the form, not so much of any kind of conscious Russian nationalism or populism, as of a very distinctive, accessible neo-classicism. Eighteenth-century ideals are invoked in the use of "sonata form"—at least its external shell—in the triadic harmonic structure, in the use of simple accompaniment figures of the "Alberti bass" type, in the simple rhythmic and phrase structures, and in the character of the cadence. The classical cadence is very important in Prokofiev's style; he uses it as a point of reference, as a local articulation, to clarify a constant series of sideslips into distant keys. These cycles of keys, often very loosely related and only briefly touched upon, give Prokofiev's music its characteristic sound—diatonic but constantly "modulating."

In spite of the composer's modification of his style in the direction of clarity and simplicity, his music remained under frequent attack in the Soviet Union for reasons which must remain obscure to Western observers; perhaps its lack of overtly nationalist character was a factor. Nevertheless, there are many points of correspondence between Prokofiev's development and that of Stravinsky—not to mention younger Russian emigré composers like Alexander Tcherepnin (b. 1899) and Nicolas Nabokov (b. 1903)—and it seems reasonable to speak of a Russian tradition of "neo-classicism" of which Prokofiev's music forms a distinctive part. As with Stravinsky, Prokofiev's artistic choices were careful and conscious; unlike Stravinsky, he never succeeded in finding new and organic forms for either his new or his neo-classical ideas and ideals; the attraction of his work ultimately lies in qualities like the lyrical character of the invention and, in his earlier compositions, the strong, motoric character of the musical motion.

Prokofiev's musical personality was largely formed before the Revolution of 1917. Of the younger composers whose careers coincide with the advent of the Communist regime, only three have more than a local significance: the Armenian, Aram Khatchaturian (b. 1903), Dmitri Kabalevsky (b. 1904), and Dmitri Shostakovitch (b. 1906). The first two have upheld the ideals of a musical populism superficially based on folk material but amplified in a big, colorful, late-romantic, bourgeois, symphonic manner. Shostakovitch is, however, a far more original and distinctive musical personality whose career and development have been—rather unfortunately— closely identified with the political and esthetic vicissitudes of Soviet life in the last forty years; Shostakovitch himself has declared on several occasions that his art has a "political basis" and he has consistently accepted political and social criticism of his work, even to the point of repudiating publicly many of his compositions.

Shostakovitch's orientation was, from the first, "neo-classic" and tonal, with a primary bias towards a simple, symphonic idiom. As with many of the later works of Prokofiev, the classical starting point for Shostakovitch is Beethoven (from the viewpoint of Soviet Marxist criticism, Beethoven was the first "socialist realist" composer). But Shostakovitch's individuality grows out of the contrast between an extended, almost sentimental lyricism and a vigorous, grotesque, dissonant wit—stylistic characteristics which have apparently not always resulted in music consonant with the dictates of official taste. (To the extent that Shostakovitch's genius runs to parody and grotesquerie, the conflict is clearer from a Western point of view than the similar controversy over Prokofiev's music.) Shostakovitch's First Symphony, the work that first brought him to world-wide attention and still possibly his most remarkable composition, is a lean, hard piece of music full of mordant wit; it is like a caricature of the classical symphony (unlike Prokofiev's similar early work which is executed with respect and affection for the traditional form). At this time, the Russian modernists were closely in touch with developments in Western music, and there is no doubt that Shostakovitch was acquainted with and influenced by German and French art. His opera, *The Nose*, based on Gogol (1927–1928), *The Golden Age* ballet of 1929– 1930, and the famous *Lady Macbeth of the Mtsensk District* of 1930–1932 are brilliant works of the most intense, satiric sort. Even in the composer's Second Symphony of 1927, dedicated to the October Revolution, there are the strong, intense, biting chromaticism, hard rhythmic edges, and lean, brittle orchestral sound with which Shostakovitch made his mark and which brought him so many difficulties.

A visit by Stalin to *Lady Macbeth* marked the beginning of trouble. Shostakovitch was bitterly attacked in the press; both the opera and the Fourth Symphony, then in rehearsal, were withdrawn. A ballet about a collectivist farm was not good enough; the manner was still too lean, too stylized for the socialist taste. Only with the Fifth Symphony of 1937 did Shostakovitch redeem himself; and thereafter he devoted himself in his major works largely to a new synthetic, heroic style. The influence of Mahler, already present in compositions like the withdrawn Fourth Symphony, became the basis of a whole series of long, long symphonic works of enormous size and pretension: the Seventh ("Leningrad"); the long, ambitious Eighth; the Twelfth, also dedicated to the Revolution; and so forth.

In addition to the usual patriotic cantatas, Shostakovitch has composed a great deal of incidental music for the theatre and the films. He has also written concertos for piano and for two pianos—clattering, breezy, ironic, jaunty works—and a quantity of solo piano and chamber music of simple, almost elementary musical qualities. The classicism and directness of the eight or nine string quartets have commanded admiration in some quarters, but the thinness and timidity of the conceptions seem to suggest that the spareness of the medium and the range of its possibilities put it out of Shostakovitch's reach. He remains primarily a symphonist, secondarily a dramatist (*Lady Macbeth* has been produced again under the title *Katerina Ismailova*, and *The Nose* has had much success recently in Europe). His large structures, built on long, simple tonal planes, endless repetition, rhythmic and harmonic insistence, and big dramatic contrasts spaced out on a Mahlerian time scale, are not profound though they generally affect the appearance of profundity. Nevertheless they do achieve, almost by sheer force of will, a certain scope and grandeur.

Northern Europe: Scandinavia

Leaving aside the late-romantic Danish composer, Carl Nielsen (1865–1931), who was touched by neo-classicism in his later work, the only important Scandinavian composer who can be considered here is Jean Sibelius (1865–1957). Sibelius's position in twentieth-century music is an odd one; he is a rare example of a composer of this century who evolved a notably original style out of nineteenth-century methods and conceptions. He began at the end of the 1800's as a composer of salon music, fashionable tone poems, and a First Symphony of a strongly Tchaikovskyian cast. In a large number of songs, solo piano and solo string works, Sibelius remained essentially—like Tchaikovsky in his smaller works—a salon composer of trivial taste. Only in a few of these compositions and, particularly, in choruses, where something of a folk character predominates, does the music take on a little more profile—even if the profile sometimes resembles Grieg.[1] The tone poems too, in spite of their dark and impressive color and unmistakably personal style, are works of limited means, full of the grand gestures of the German and Slavic Romantic masters spruced up a bit and made to do service for Finnish mythology.

Aside from a string quartet, *Voces Intimae* (1909), and the Violin Concerto (1903), Sibelius's significant development must be traced in his seven symphonies, written over a period of twenty-five years, between 1899 and 1924. The Second Symphony of 1901 and, to a lesser extent, the Third of a few years later, show a strong handling of traditional materials; but the most original of the series is the Fourth, written in 1911 —the period of the great musical upheavals on the continent. The personal crisis in Sibelius's music was also, in part, a tonal crisis. The Fourth Symphony centers on the ambiguous interval of the augmented fourth, and from its opening measures until some point near the end, the tonal resolution of the piece is in doubt. The remarkable thing about this work, aside from its moody and dissonant character, is its strong conception of form generated organically out of the musical ideas. The ideas come in fragments, and the formal process—almost the reverse of traditional developmental conceptions—is one of gradual cohesion; the fragments merge and resolve into coherent tonal structures of considerable power. None of Sibelius's later symphonies—the Fifth in 1914–1915 and the last two dating from the 1920's—shows anything like the harmonic, melodic, and orchestral originality of the Fourth, and Sibelius returned to firmer tonal ground in these later works. But they share his typical halting, expressive, organic, tonal symphonic form which, in the traditional sense, had other-tortured kind of musical speech; and they retain—and even in the Seventh expand—this remarkable "synthetic" technique, preserving a sense of big, wise vanished.

Northern Europe: England

England, like the countries of Eastern and Northern Europe, was a long-time cultural dependency of Central Europe which finally established a measure of independence and national idiom partly through folk style. Sir Edward Elgar (1857–1934) was a late and somewhat provincial representative of the great symphonic tradition, and both Gustav Holst (1874–1934) and Delius—two of the most important creative musicians in the

---

[1] There are among the songs a few works of a spare and striking character in a class with the best of his symphonic music.

development of English musical life in the early part of the century—had Central European parental and musical antecedents. Delius, as previously noted, was attracted by the new French style with its floating, suspended sense of tonality and its exaltation of timbre as a basic expressive and formal means of musical expression. Delius's "impressionism" has individuality, but the first composer to use these techniques in a distinctly English manner was Ralph Vaughan Williams (1872–1958). Like Delius, Vaughan Williams was brought up in the classical-romantic Central European tradition, both in England where it was dominant and in Germany where he studied with Max Bruch. Later, like Bartók, he began to collect folk songs; still later, he studied with Maurice Ravel. These facts are not unconnected. Vaughan Williams was never an "impressionist" in any meaningful sense, but impulses from old English music—including Tudor art music, also pre-tonal in its basis—combined with "impressionist," harmonic, and coloristic techniques to form a personal and indisputably English style. After the early vocal works and fantasias on folk and Tudor themes, actual quotation of old English music is not prominent in Vaughan Williams's music, but—in a minor way, as in the case of Bartók—the double experience of pre- and post-tonal music made possible the formation of a distinctive style, anchored in some kind of modal-tonality but free of the traditional tonal way of thinking. Vaughan Williams's later work is characterized by an expansion and consolidation of technique and style in an attempt to create a large-scale English symphonic manner, with new tonal techniques enclosed in adaptations of traditional forms. This big symphonic style, characteristic of English twentieth-century music, particularly in the 1930's—see Arnold Bax (1883–1953), Arthur Bliss (b. 1891), and William Walton (b. 1902)—is not unrelated to parallel Russian and Scandinavian developments, and it is significant that composers like Shostakovitch, Sibelius, and Nielsen have always been notably well received in England.

The development of the big modern English symphonic (and vocal) style—even in the strongest and most original works of Vaughan Williams—moved steadily towards an evocation of a full romantic style; at the same time, however, England developed a strong classical strain of considerable originality. The initial impulse came from France—from the Paris of Stravinsky and "Les Six"; indeed, the piano music and ballet scores of Lord Berners (1883–1950) were written for and produced in the French capital. The most important English production of this period was Walton's *Façade*, a setting of Edith Sitwell poems declaimed (originally by Miss Sitwell herself) to the witty, agile commentary of a chamber orchestra. Walton later abandoned the free, lean, dissonant, chamber style of the work to turn towards a more neutral, accessible, "English" symphonic style. (Significantly, he later romanticized *Façade* in a ballet version scored for large orchestra.)

The most important and original English neo-tonal music is that of

Benjamin Britten. Britten, who was born in 1913, developed under the influence of the art of Stravinsky and the French, but he has been able to strike a distinctive and original note. Britten's fundamental idiom is based on a synthetic tonal technique elucidated with great simplicity, naturalness, and skillful clarity growing out of a kind of melodic thinking which is often vocal in origin. Britten has also responded to English tradition—the tradition of Purcell and of English choral music, rather than that of the folk song or Elizabethan madrigal—but any specifically English quality which can be ascribed to his music is the result of its force of character rather than of any easily isolated musical features. Britten has never hesitated to use—and often with conspicuous success—a wide range of musical techniques integrated by means of simple, artful, new tonal forms. His forms are nearly always, in spite of appearances, highly constructed; a problem is that they are not always organic. The music is typically put together in freely diatonic melodic-vocal phrases, often set into a simple contrapuntal web and punctuated by clipped, highly colored, triadic harmonies. The basic long-range motion, the big structure, and even ultimately the sense of convincing tonal organization depend, however, on a careful inner manipulation of relationships functioning at another and far less simple level than the attractive and easily apprehended exterior. This odd, double construction is not difficult to detect in works like the opera *The Turn of the Screw* (1953-1954)—based on a twelve-tone "row" which is simply a cycle of fourths—or the *War Requiem* (1963) where the opposition of levels and the transformation of intellectual and musical materials actually operate as a kind of intellectual drama beneath the more obvious Stravinsky-Verdi dramatic surface.

Any list of Britten's major compositions will serve to indicate the importance of the human voice in his work; his three big choral-orchestral works—the *Sinfonia da Requiem* (1940), the *Spring Symphony* (1949) and the *War Requiem*—and smaller conceptions like *Les Illuminations* (1939; Rimbaud settings for tenor and strings), the *Serenade* for tenor, horn, and strings (1943), *Rejoice in the Lamb* (1943; to a text by Christopher Smart), and *A Ceremony of Carols* (1942) are among his most successful pieces. Finally, his stage works, referred to later, are strongly oriented towards lyric-intellectual as well as purely dramatic expressions. Except for an "occasional" work like *Noye's Fludde* (1959), with its children's orchestra of carillonneurs and recorder players, and the more recent *Curlew River*, they are within the framework of conventional operatic gesture and plan; nevertheless, they represent the first important English operas since Purcell's, and containing as they do some of Britten's best music, they serve to confirm the vocal basis of his art.

Britten's music became the natural starting point for younger English composers, but with the limited exception of Michael Tippett, there has been no strong personality who has been able to develop in this direction. As nearly everywhere else, classicism and neo-tonality have been turned aside by or absorbed into chromatic styles, and even Britten has cautiously expanded his own techniques to utilize ideas from serial and even post-serial music.

Southern Europe: Italy and Spain

In spite of the great role that Italy played in the establishment of the classical tradition, there was a complete break in the tradition in every field except opera. After 1900, Italian instrumental and even vocal music had to renew itself in a manner not so different from that of East Europe, Scandinavia, and England. The difference—and it is an important one—is that the Italians did not strike out anew from folk music but rather from their Renaissance and Baroque traditions.

There were two Italians with strong musical connections with the nineteenth century who were touched by new ideas. One, Ferruccio Busoni (1866–1924), actually anticipated many important contemporary ideas in his remarkable writings about music, although as a composer he participated in the century's revolutions only to a limited degree; in any case, his work belongs largely to Central European musical life and had only small influence in his native country. The other, Giacomo Puccini (1858–1924), is an extraordinary case of a brilliant and successful composer in a conservative tradition who consciously enriched his own means of expression with new ideas: from the parallel fifths in *La Bohème* (1896) to the Debussyisms of *Il Tabarro* (1918) and the striking dissonances of *Turandot* (1924; completed by Franco Alfano), his operatic style continually assimilated techniques which were essentially outside the conventional operatic apparatus. Puccini's tonal-vocal style is contemporary in this essential respect, and its influence is still great in the theatre and in popular music.

A definitive break with the operatic tradition and the establishment of a new Italian symphonic-tonal—and, later, also vocal-operatic—style was accomplished by a younger group of composers including Casella (already discussed above in connection with neo-classicism), Ottorino Respighi (1879–1936), Ildebrando Pizzetti (b. 1880) and Gianfrancesco Malipiero (b. 1882). Respighi, a kind of modern Italian Rimsky-Korsakov (with whom he actually studied), was a sensualist who synthesized a sackful of sure-fire ingredients ranging from Gregorian chant to Rimsky-Korsakov and Debussy, all done up in a brilliant, popular manner. Respighi's popularity rests on a small group of orchestral works, although the bulk of his output is to be found in more than a dozen operatic compositions, all failures. With the exception of Casella, all of these Italians made extensive attempts to revive and renovate Italian opera with a new and modern tonal technique based on free and wide-ranging diatonic elements, essentially unrelated to recent Italian operatic tradition but nonetheless distinctively Italian in their particular adaptation of contemporary ideas. The bulk of Pizzetti's work, outside of his songs, belongs in this category; the results, whatever their intrinsic musical merit, have not been notably successful.

Of this group of composers, undoubtedly the most important is Malipiero, whose long list of compositions includes a number of stage pieces (including the attractive and occasionally performed Goldoni triptych written in 1919–1921) and an even more extensive catalogue of instrumental and orchestral works. Malipiero's free diatonic technique, strongly imbued with a kind of vocally derived counterpoint, a mild use of dissonance, and rather improvisatory lyric-dramatic forms, contains scarcely a trace of anything that could be described as local color; the basic wandering modal character of the "tonal" writing has nothing to do with folk music. However, Malipiero strikes a distinctively Italian note due in part to his derivations from pre-tonal Italian music, particularly the great vocal tradition up through Monteverdi.

In contrast to the rather reserved, simple, but almost aristocratic ideals of the new Italian art music (of the group after Puccini which attempted to renovate vocal ideals and synthesize them with a new instrumental music, only Respighi developed a really popular idiom), the revival of Spanish music, in large part the creation of the composer Felipe Pedrell (1841–1922), was consciously and thoroughly based on traditional music. The familiar elements of this tradition, derived largely from an aural performance style,[2] consist principally of some fairly complex rhythmic patterns within a steady and obsessive metrical frame, and a rich and highly ornamented melos based on a few characteristic modal patterns—of obviously Eastern origin—to which have been added or adapted a few simple Western harmonies. The extensive transformation of this material into "art" music is almost entirely due to the harmonic developments in French music at the end of the nineteenth and the beginning of the twentieth centuries. Some of the most important use of Spanish material occurs in the work of Debussy and Ravel, and composers like Albéniz (1860–1909) and Granados (1867–1916) were closely influenced by the "impressionists" (also by d'Indy, Fauré, and Dukas). Debussy, Ravel, and later, Stravinskyian "neo-classicism" were also starting points for Manuel de Falla (1876–1946), not merely because Falla had no native precedents on which to base a new, Spanish style but also because the new materials of French music could give form to other characteristic ideas without wrenching them into the conventions of the old tonal system. Two of Falla's best-known pieces are concerted works: *Nights in the Gardens of Spain* for piano and orchestra (1909–1915) and the Concerto for harpsichord and chamber ensemble (1923–1926), the latter the most obviously "neo-classical" of his works. There are also piano pieces and vocal works including the *Seven Spanish Popular Songs*, one of the surprisingly rare examples of the actual use of Spanish folk material in Falla's music. Falla's

[2] Partly Gypsy and partly Spanish-Arabic in origin.

most important work, however, was for the theatre; it ranges from the colorful, florid Spanish style of the opera *La Vida breve* (1904–5) and the ballet *El Amor brujo* (1915) to the drier, wittier neo-classicism of *El Retablo de Maese Pedro* (1919), a scenic play with puppets, adapted from an episode in *Don Quixote,* and the attempted synthesis of the large, unfinished *Atlántida.*

The range of Falla's activity framed nearly all of the work produced in Spain for many years from Ernesto Halffter (b. 1905), the most Stravinskyian of the Spaniards, to local-color composers like Joaquín Turina (1882–1949), Joaquín Nin (1879–1949), Joaquín Rodrigo (b. 1902), and others. Only recently and with great reluctance have Spanish composers begun to abandon Spanish tradition as a primary source of musical ideas and forms, and although the younger composers in Spain—as everywhere else—are now committed to chromaticism, serialism, and beyond, one can still find attempts to synthesize new with traditional materials *à la* Bartók or even shotgun marriages of *cante hondo* and serialism *à la* Boulez.

Latin America

The impulse which produced the remarkable Mexican pictorial school in the 1920's also generated a new Mexican music of significance. Like the painting, this music was liberated by the new techniques and new freedoms produced in Europe at the beginning of the century but it developed—only up to a point, to be sure—in a distinctive way. A composer like Carlos Chávez (b. 1899) benefited, like many of his colleagues in the United States at the time, from the opportunity to develop an intense original musicality at a long distance from the old tradition. Chávez's early works are his radical ones; in his free use of percussion, in the intense, linear, chromatic expressive angularity and dissonance of a work like the ballet *Antígona* (1932; 1940) in the remarkable use of percussion in works like the *Sinfonía India* (1935) and the *Toccata* for percussion (1947), in the driving power of works like the ballet *HP* (i.e., horsepower) (1932), Chávez established a musical line of expression which was both contemporary and national without being narrowly folkloristic. Nevertheless, in spite of the composer's awareness of the limitations of mere folklorism, Chávez was inevitably involved—as were his painter contemporaries—in social consciousness and social expression. For Rivera and Orozco, this meant a focus on subject matter and interpretation of the social situation; for Chávez it meant clarified tonal techniques and direct communicativeness without or (preferably) with folklore. From this point, Chávez later turned to big symphonic and classical-romantic tonal form.

The most curious figure of the Mexican musical renaissance was Silvestre Revueltas (1899–1940), who, in the brief span of forty-one years, produced an *oeuvre* in which an actual or imagined Indian-Mexican music of primitive intensity was put together with a kind of obsessive, *Sacre du Printemps* technique. Revueltas's music is like much other experimental music of the period—not quite fully realized. The Cuban composer Amadeo Roldán (1900–1939) is a similar case; like Revueltas he was a talented extremist and his *Rítmicas* V and VI are possibly the first works written for an all-percussion ensemble (they precede Varèse's *Ionisation* by a year or two). Like Revueltas, Roldán died young, before his talents were fully realized.

The North American tradition of experimentalism did not extend to South America, although the southern continent's one really important composer, Heitor Villa-Lobos (1887–1959), remained a considerable distance from European tradition in temperament and style. A Brazilian, Villa-Lobos had a natural affinity with modern French music (Milhaud's stay in Brazil in 1917–1919 as French cultural attaché had an important influence in introducing him to Debussy and other modern French music); any rough description of Villa-Lobos's music would have to contend with "Les Six," Brazilian-Portuguese-African folk and popular style, "impressionism," especially in the instrumental usage, a bit of Indian music, and a touch of jazz. Villa-Lobos began his musical career playing in café orchestras; essentially self-taught as a composer, he was one of the most prolific—and uncritical—musicians who ever lived. The result is an enormous mass of music, tossed off with great ease and freedom, often utterly charming, very often trivial, sometimes utterly confused and inconsistent, sometimes impressive. Tonality was as natural a technique to Villa-Lobos as it was to the street musicians who provided the model for the ditties he loved so well; but his tonality is often clouded by huge masses of rich sound color applied liberally with the palette knife and without much care. Perhaps the best—or at least the most characteristic—of Villa-Lobos's music is to be found in the various works titled *Chôros* and *Bachianas Brasileiras* written over a period of more than twenty-five years.

Among younger South Americans, only the Argentinian Alberto Ginastera (b. 1916) has produced important work in a national-tonal tradition. His ballets, *Panambí* (1940) and *Estancia* (1941), have the now-classical Indian-Latin-*Rite-of-Spring* mixture but his later music is atonal-serial in the post-war mode.

The United States

In another volume of this series, twentieth-century music in the United States is discussed in the context of the American past and of American tradition. It remains here—and elsewhere in this volume—to discuss the position of music in the United States vis-à-vis the international development of contemporary style. Certainly the first attempts to estab-

lish a new tonal, "national" style completely outside the tradition of functional tonality must be ascribed—along with so many other things—to
Charles Ives (1874–1954), but Ives is perhaps more fruitfully considered
along with the great American experimental and avant-garde movements
discussed below. In several important and individual ways, the vast
changes in European music during the first part of the century were
paralleled—sometimes anticipated, sometimes followed—in the United
States. Similarly, the development of new tonal styles and the new musical
nationalisms in the 1920's, 1930's, and 1940's were paralleled—and, because
of the war, often developed and continued—in this country. The new preoccupations with the relationship of the composer to the musical com-
munity, the public, and society; the brave attempt to reintegrate the creative artist into his society through musical populism, music for use, school
music, worker's music, and songs for the masses; the preoccupation with
the use of recordings, radio, theatre, and films as a means for reaching a
mass audience; the phenomenal success of Kurt Weill and the interest
in music as a vehicle for social commentary; the mystique of purposeful-
ness and utilitarianism; the search for a national music combined with the
revived interest in national, popular, and folk expression—all had a profound effect on this side of the Atlantic. Ironically, at the very moment
when the United States had to assume most of the burden of international
contemporary musical life, its composers were looking inward and backward trying to find a specifically American musical identity.

The initial impulses for this new American tonal music came from
Stravinsky and the French, to a lesser extent from Hindemith, and in the
theatre, from Kurt Weill. Stravinsky's neo-classic "idea" appeared as a
stylistic vessel which could carry many different kinds of contents: jazz
as well as Bach, a folk tune as well as a neo-Mozartian melody. Roger
Sessions's First Symphony (1927), Aaron Copland's "Jazz" Concerto for
piano and orchestra (1926), and a whole host of works by lesser composers—nearly all of whom studied how to make first-class neo-tonality
with Nadia Boulanger in Paris—Americanized these techniques with skill
and ease. A composer like Virgil Thomson (b. 1896), with his attitudes of
elegance and artful simplicity, reduced such ideas to their absolute essentials: disassociated scales and triads treated exactly like the dissociated
words and phrases in the texts of Gertrude Stein which he employed.

The center of this activity in the 1930's and early 1940's was the
theatre and related media. After a period of working with chromatic and
even serial techniques, Copland (b. 1900) developed his popular style in
the well-known series of ballets. George Gershwin (1898–1937; the first
actual arrival from the world of popular music); Marc Blitzstein (1905–
1964; an intellectual convert from highbrow music); Thomson; the
quickly Americanized Kurt Weill; and others scored real theatrical
successes. Copland, George Antheil (1900–1959), Louis Gruenberg (1884–
1964), and Paul Bowles (b. 1910) wrote movie music; and there was a

considerable activity on the four radio networks, which sponsored a great deal of new music of the more popular sort. This was also the period of innumerable symphonic "Hoedowns" and "Square Dances" as well as of the growth of a broad, serious, symphonic style, strongly tonal (generally in a Stravinskyian or modal sort of way), based on traditional patterns often rather awkwardly arranged to fit the new local-color material; influenced by Stravinsky, Hindemith, and the Soviet composers but—in one way or another—definably American. The idea was, more or less, to adapt the great tradition to a New World style for the large, new American public—in short, to write "The Great American Symphony." Copland himself produced important music in this vein—notably his Third Symphony (1946) and his more ascetic Piano Sonata (1939–1941)—but the best and most consistent representative of the style was perhaps Roy Harris (b. 1898). Harris's works—notably his Third Symphony (1938) and his Piano Quintet (1936)—seem to have lost ground in recent years, but in their day they were considered models of serious style and form combined with clear, handsome, and accessible ideas that were identifiably American. The "American" character of these works—and many others on the same model—is only partly due to the actual use of folk or folk-popular material. Certain types of stylized, expressive melody, popular in origin but much transformed—a simple, halting motion, in scale steps within a small diatonic compass or in wide leaps of fourths and fifths, with metrical changes based on alternating threes and twos, and with a certain amount of syncopation—became hallmarks, along with wide, open harmonies built on major seconds, fourths, and fifths and a flat, colorful, open orchestration. The three- and four-movement forms were—except in the dance and theatre pieces—almost invariably and rather uncomfortably borrowed from traditional patterns.

By no means all of the American symphonic music of this type was restricted to this model; it was just that the model was the most typical, distinctive, and obviously American. Conservative composers like Howard Hanson (b. 1896) and Samuel Barber (b. 1910) have remained closer or returned to European prototypes, particularly those derived from Romantic symphonic literature. On the other hand, William Schuman (b. 1910) has been involved in a much wider range of materials in his development of a big symphonic style based on chromatic ideas, a rich, dissonant harmonic material, high powered rhythmic impulse and orchestration, and structures which come out of these materials. The music of Walter Piston (b. 1894) belongs somewhere in between; highly polished, basically diatonic in its orientation, and strongly dependent on classical models, it remains poised between ideals of serious, classical workmanship and high degrees of tension and articulation.

The generation of composers whose work became known in the 1930's and 1940's can be divided—a little too neatly perhaps—between those who attempted to carry forward some kind of development of the "American School" popular-symphonic idea—like David Diamond (b. 1915), Peter Mennin (b. 1923), William Flanagan (b. 1926)—and those who were working towards a lively American "neo-classical" style full of elegance, wit, and resonance—Arthur Berger (b. 1912), Irving Fine (1914–1963), Elliott Carter (b. 1908), and Lukas Foss (b. 1922). The former style has remained rather constant in the new works of older composers (occasionally showing twelve-tone influence) and it is essentially without influence on the younger generation; the latter has evolved into or been completely superseded by serial or other avant-garde developments.

There remains one composer, Ernest Bloch (1880–1959), who must be considered here—partly for want of a better place and partly because he spent most of his creative life in the United States. In spite of the fact that Bloch wrote a large symphonic work, *America* (1926), employing American folksongs, hymns, and even jazz, he can hardly be considered an American composer, and indeed, in spite of his well-known works on Hebrew motifs, he cannot be accurately or meaningfully classified as a Jewish composer. Bloch was born in Switzerland, studied in Belgium, lived in Paris and—after 1916—in the United States. He was a composer rooted in the Central European late romantic tradition; in spite of some important vocal works, he was oriented towards a symphonic style covered with literary and poetic trappings. His early style is an amalgam of Debussy, Richard Strauss, and Mahler, to which he later adapted the expanded vocabulary of early twentieth-century modernism and even—in the mode of Honegger or Kodály—a certain amount of neo-classicism. Bloch was certainly not without influence on the development of American music, but he was a strong eclectic with an extremely various and uneven production that remains difficult to pigeon-hole.

Bibliography

The literature on local style is enormous and spread out in a multitude of languages. The standard Bartók book in English is that of Halsey Stevens (New York, 1953, 2nd edition, 1965); there is a major Hungarian study by Bence Szabolcsi published in Budapest in French (*Bartók: Sa Vie et son oeuvre*, 1952). See also the studies of the Bartók String Quartets by Milton Babbitt (*Musical Quarterly*, July, 1949) and Matyas Seiber (London, 1945); Allan Forte's analysis of part of the Fourth Quartet appears in the *Problems of Modern Music* issue of *The Musical Quarterly* (April, 1960). For Russian and Soviet composers, see Gerald Abraham's *Eight Soviet Composers*, London, 1948. Israel Nestyev's *Prokofiev* (Eng. tr., New York, 1946) is distorted by its "Soviet"—not to say Stalinist—point of view; Pierre Souvtchinsky's *Musique russe*, already mentioned, is a useful corrective. For Sibelius, see the symposium edited by Gerald Abraham (*Music of Sibelius*, New York, 1947). There is an excellent book on Benjamin Britten's earlier works by Hans Keller and Donald Mitchell (London, 1953). For Chávez, see the composer's own *Musical*

Thought (Norton Poetry Lectures of 1958–1959; published by Harvard, 1960). For comments on the development of neo-classic and neo-tonal styles in American music, see the author's own article *"Modern Music* in Retrospect" in the Spring–Summer, 1964, issue of *Perspectives of New Music;* see also Henry Cowell's *American Composers on American Music* (1933, reprinted New York, 1962), Aaron Copland's collected articles *On Music* (New York, 1960, but containing articles dating from 1926 on), Wilfrid Mellers's English view in *Music in a New Found Land* (London, 1964), and H. Wiley Hitchcock's *Music in the United States: A Historical Introduction* in the Prentice-Hall History of Music Series.

9

Musical Theatre

Musical theatre ought not to be considered apart from the general development of musical creativity; but it must unfortunately be so treated in any discussion of twentieth-century music. For the first time since the origins of modern opera around 1600, the theatre has ceased to be a primary generating creative force in musical style; it has remained by and large essentially conservative, closely dependent on traditional ideas of vocal writing and operatic routine. Furthermore, in spite of an enormous amount of promise and a great deal of experimentation, new theatrical ideas and techniques have not lent themselves well to adaptation through new musical ideas, and the use of music in the new dramatic media—films, radio, television—has (again in spite of a great deal of promise) remained secondary and derivative. Only a single theatrical medium has been consistently and closely identified with new and creative musical developments: the dance. This successful union has, however, been characterized in great part by a development of dance itself away from dramatic forms towards more lyric or more intellectual—in short, more abstract—conceptions. All of this should not be taken to mean that contemporary theatre has been without musical importance, and it is possible that avant-garde musical materials and forms will find a proper expression in some kind of new theatre when the relationships between the new theatrical and musical means and experiences are better understood.

Puccini and verismo

The operas of Giacomo Puccini might seem scarcely to fall within the scope of this study at all, but *Turandot*—left unfinished at the composer's death in 1924—is the last opera to enter the international repertory and one of the few in that repertory to employ definitively twentieth-century melodic, harmonic, and orchestral techniques. French "impressionism" produced comparatively little for the stage, although assuredly three masterpieces in Debussy's *Pelléas et Mélisande* (1892–1902) and Ravel's charming one-act operas *L'Heure espagnole* (1907) and *L'Enfant et les sortilèges* (1924–1925). But as early as *La Bohème* (1896), Puccini began to come under the influence of Debussyian harmonic ideas. In spite of its origins in the Italian tradition, Puccini's melodic technique, with its "modal" turns of phrase, is essentially twentieth-century in conception, and his harmonic-melodic conceptions are often quite surprisingly free—in implication at least—of traditional functional-tonal prejudices. Thus, the series of unrelated triads at the beginning of *Tosca*, the parallel fifths that open the third act of *La Bohème*, the tonal irresolution of the end of *Madama Butterfly*, the dabs of detached harmonic and orchestral color at the beginning of *Il Tabarro*, and the sequences of parallel seventh and ninth chords that appear in the later works are by no means isolated usages. Puccini's rather flexible diatonic melodic style (often curiously modal or pentatonic, even in the non-oriental operas) combines with a rich and free harmonic style based on piled-up thirds, parallel motion, and dramatic harmonic and tonal shifts to form a consistent musical style distinct from traditional practice, closely interwoven with the dramatic conceptions, and distinctly twentieth-century in character. Puccini's greatest influence was on the development of popular musical theatre, film music, and—to a lesser degree—on certain related, lighter forms of jazz. Parallel sequences of ninth and eleventh chords, first extensively employed by Puccini as a way of enriching the support of a simple modal or diatonic melodic line, have become clichés of popular-song harmonization. In theatrical idea and form, Puccini was not an innovator although his type of musical theatre—as well as his musical style—has been much imitated. In general, the late operas of Verdi provide the models: set numbers of the classical type alternate with narrative or dialogue scenes, the whole framed in a continuous and prominent orchestral texture; indeed the orchestra often carries the entire musical motion and significance, with the vocal parts reduced to a simple, word-conveying *parlando*, sometimes built on the mere repetition of one or two tones. Puccini's contemporaries, Leoncavallo and Mascagni, introduced a popular or local subject-matter in their operas, which thus pass under the name of "verismo." Puccini's material, however, is far more wide-ranging—often exotic in a kind of *fin de siècle* way and always reflecting the theatrical taste of his period: *Tosca* (1900), *Madama Butterfly* (1904), and *The Girl of the Golden West* (1910) were based on popular plays of the time; *La Bohème* and *Il Tabarro* derive from scenes of contemporary life. Only in *Turandot*, a curious fantasy-comedy by the eighteenth-century Italian, Gozzi, did Puccini venture to treat a dramatic concept essentially removed from the missing-fourth-wall realistic theatre concept. *Turandot* is a mythic, symbolic theatre of masks, and its music—highly colored, full of dissonant accent, often tonally ambiguous—is equally far from tonal "realism."

Nearly all of Puccini's contemporaries—Giordano, Mascagni, Leoncavallo—bogged down in the almost impossible task of creating a significant operatic parallel to the literary realism of Sardou or Verga. The remarkable success of *Cavalleria Rusticana* and *I Pagliacci* and the exceptional ability of Puccini to overcome the inherent contradictions in the so-called realistic opera (which even Puccini deserted at the end of his life) misled a great many composers into thinking that a popular post-Puccini style was possible; it was not. Outside of the world of musical comedy, Puccini's operatic style has had dozens of imitators and few consequents of note: *Porgy and Bess* and the operas of Menotti. Gershwin's *Porgy* (1935) stands apart; it remains, in spite of its ambitions, a masterpiece of musical comedy—not necessarily an inferior or less significant category at all but one which demands consideration under a different heading. The Puccini-ism of Gian-Carlo Menotti (b. 1911) is not merely musical: Menotti thinks of musical theatre in terms of function, space, dramatic incident, and structure in exactly the way that Puccini did, even when the two composers' subjects are most divergent. Menotti's theatre is not always "realistic," but it is certainly contemporary in its subject matter and its concerns; his particular musical talent enables him to create orchestral and vocal parts which do not hinder, and sometimes heighten, the dramatic context.

The Wagnerian tradition and expressionist opera

For all the significance of "The Music of the Future" at the end of the nineteenth and the beginning of the twentieth century, the essentials of the Wagnerian theatrical concept remained more or less the exclusive property of Wagner. A great many "Wagnerian" operas were written in Wagner's day and afterwards; none of them need concern us here. The possibilities of a development in the operatic theatre out of the direct inheritance of Wagnerian style are represented—indeed exhausted—in the work of a single composer, Richard Strauss. As we have seen, Strauss extended Wagnerian contrapuntal chromaticism to the edge of atonality in *Salome* and *Elektra* and then backed away. The rich orchestral and vocal web of *Der Rosenkavalier* is Wagnerian in technique but classical and tonal in subject matter; from a certain point of view, *Ariadne auf Naxos* is actually a long dialogue—a conjunction of oppositions—concerning expressive freedom and classical form. Strauss's later operas are often concerned with this kind of opposition, an aspect which enhances their contemporary intellectual interest but which weakens them in the theatre. His later musical style coalesces around an expanded contrapuntal tonality, diatonic and even functional in the old way, but freely moving with shifting triads and seventh chords sliding through the entire chromatic range; it is a kind of super-enharmonic diatonicism in which all the implications of chromaticism are present, not necessarily in detail at all, but on a grand scale.

The later operas of Strauss, whatever their final value may be, stand apart from the mainstreams of twentieth-century development; *Salome* and *Elektra*, on the other hand, are key works. Aside from the huge apparatus of post-Wagnerian technique, these dramas are remarkable for their concentration of means and materials and their penetrating psychological subject-matter. The two aspects—which are not unrelated—mark a fundamental departure from the Wagnerian esthetic—which is slow, developmental, and narrative in plan, schematic and mythic in subject matter. Where Wagner may use 136 measures to unfold and explicate an idea as simple as a tonic triad (in the prelude to *Das Rheingold*), Strauss concentrates a whole mass of conflicting motives, a dense, contrasting harmonic motion, and elaborate rhythmic and orchestral textures into a relatively few minutes; what happens in Wagner as a sequence of events occurs in Strauss as simultaneities or as a quick dialogue of opposites. From this point of view, *Salome* and, especially, *Elektra* are difficult works to hear; they seem to be full of unsorted detail, of half-phrases without consequents, of tensions and energies never fully released. In a sense, the big shape of these works is neither a musical form nor, in the conventional sense, a dramatic one; the structure of both (excluding the irrelevant and banal insertion of "The Dance of the Seven Veils" in *Salome*) is psychological. Such a concentrated psychological form with its word-for-word setting, its constant opposition of conflicting elements, and its rapid, intense pulse does not really exist in Wagner although its strictly musical techniques may seem at first to be superficially Wagnerian; Wagner perhaps only approached it in isolated sections like Tristan's monologue at the beginning of the last act of *Tristan und Isolde*. It exists in a limited

Richard Strauss as John the Baptist. Caricature by Georges Villa. Meyer Collection, Paris. Reproduction forbidden.

way in late Verdi, and the clearest nineteenth-century prototypes are to be found in Mussorgsky. But with Strauss the form is essentially new and, one would be tempted to say, as valid in contemporary—one would almost say Freudian—terms as the modern psychological novel. Yet Strauss quickly abandoned the genre and, in the theatre at least, the idea seems to have had only one direct and significant consequent: Schoenberg's *Erwartung* (1909) with its single character and its intense, free, associative, atonal form.

All musical form is, of course, in some sense psychological, but music resists literal verbal-psychological interpretations; the very specific psychological form and totally asymmetrical conciseness of *Erwartung* made it impossible to duplicate or use as a model. Nevertheless, the experience of this kind of form and expression—musical structure whose impulses and tensions reflect, parallel, or suggest by analogy psychological states and conflicts—had a profound effect on the music of Schoenberg and, particularly, of Alban Berg. These elements are by no means inconsiderable in Schoenberg's later operas *Die Glückliche Hand* (1913), *Von Heute auf Morgen* (1928), and even *Moses und Aron* (2 acts completed 1932; unfinished); they play essential roles in Berg's *Wozzeck* (1914–1921) and *Lulu* (1928–1934), both of which are thus transformed from mere social and symbolic documents to intense studies of the human condition. The classical forms of *Wozzeck*—the sonatas, variations, and passacaglias into which the individual scenes are molded—are not at all arbitrary but form the tight, tense frames which push against and hold in place the inner developing form of the detail. In the same way, the massive, cyclical structure of *Lulu* (poorly represented, unfortunately, by the incomplete published version) parallels the mythic and symbolic content of the work and surrounds—in a sense, realizes on another plane—the intense, personal, gruesome, scabrous, or comic detail of the work.

In the narrowest and strictest sense the art-historical term "expressionism" should be limited to the handful of Central European musical stage works which fall within the framework of a historical style—intense, internal psychological conflicts represented externally by certain violent, striking artistic materials whose very shape grows out of conflict, paradox, contradiction, and psychological conflict. Bartók's opera *Bluebeard's Castle* and his ballet-pantomime *The Miraculous Mandarin* might be included here as well as—in subject-matter rather than musical technique—Busoni's *Doktor Faust* (1916–1924). By a rather uncomfortable extension of the term, one might also include a number of important theatrical works produced between the two wars which, for all their musical differences, employ some kind of expressionist theatrical techniques—Prokofiev's *The Gambler* and *The Flaming Angel*, Shostakovitch's *Lady Macbeth of Mtsensk*, Hindemith's *Cardillac* (1926) and *Mathis der Maler*, Křenek's *Jonny spielt Auf* (1925–1926), the Kurt Weill-Bert Brecht *Mahagonny* (1927) and *The Threepenny Opera* (1928), Milhaud's *Le Pauvre Matelot* (produced first only in 1927), *Le Création du monde*, and *Christophe*

Colomb, even Louis Gruenberg's *The Emperor Jones* (1932)—they all share, at the very least, the use of anti-realistic, "expressionist" techniques to represent and communicate some kind of symbolic, social, moral, or philosophical meaning. None of these works is psychologically oriented in a profound way, just as none of them is atonal or involved in the psychological significance of new materials and new forms. They are all (except for Weill's) operatic in the usual sense and they all deal with essentially contemporary problems with means that—however tonal—are certainly of the twentieth century; nevertheless, they have all remained essentially isolated expressions.[1]

The mixed genre and chamber opera

The history of opera has often been described as a continuous struggle between the dominance of language and the dominance of music. Even more significantly, the problem of musical theatre has always been the problem of form. Every composer who writes for the theatre faces the problem of resolving his ideas in dramatic forms or self-contained musical ones. The solutions need not be mutually exclusive: Verdi's and Mozart's forms are musical but they are hardly undramatic. Nevertheless, the tendency of post-Wagnerian opera—well into the twentieth century—was towards dramatic, "expressive" structures, and this seemed, even for a composer like Schoenberg, an open road leading to the development of new forms for new ideas. Stravinsky, on the other hand, closed his forms, eliminated narrative and psychological process altogether, and created the

[1] In Central Europe, where the old, widespread operatic culture has been kept alive, a post-Wagnerian line of operatic development has been continued in a series of post-war works which attempt to fuse subject matter of contemporary interest, a non-tonal or freely tonal style with chromatic and twelve-tone techniques, long chromatic post-Wagnerian vocal lines, and an on-going musical motion punctuated by closed, interior forms, the whole generally imbued with some striking symbolic significance, or commentary on modern life or the human condition. The operas of Hans Werner Henze (b. 1926), *König Hirsch, Boulevard Solitude, Der Prinz von Homburg, Elegie für junge Liebende, The Young Lords, The Bassarids* (the last three with Auden and Kallman), belong here, although they tend strongly towards Stravinskyian formal and rhythmic structure (as well as Stravinskyian-Audenish detachment). The space-ship opera *Aniara* of the Swedish composer Karl-Birger Blomdahl (b. 1916) has had considerable success. Other composers to be considered in this category include Boris Blacher (b. 1903, *Abstract Opera No. 1, Romeo und Julia*); Wolfgang Fortner (b. 1907, *Blood Wedding*); Rolf Liebermann (b. 1910, *School for Wives*). The operas of Gottfried von Einem (b. 1918, *The Trial, Dantons Tod*) also belong here. Werner Egk (b. 1901, *Der Revisor* or *The Inspector General*) and Nicolas Nabokov (b. 1903, *The Holy Devil* with text by Stephen Spender) are more distantly related; their works have strong elements of French style. Two important American composers in this area whose work ranks with European efforts are Roger Sessions (b. 1896, *The Trial of Lucullus, Montezuma*) and Hugo Weisgall (b. 1912, *The Stronger, The Tenor, Six Characters in Search of an Author, Athaliah*); *Don Rodrigo* by the Argentinian Alberto Ginastera also belongs here.

prototype of the one really new and successful twentieth-century musical theatre to date.

One tends to overlook the fact that the larger part of Stravinsky's major works was written for the theatre. The ballet, of course, occupies the first place: the famous Diaghilev ballets—including *Pulcinella*—and later the "classical" ballets and the collaboration with Balanchine culminating in the remarkable *Agon* of 1957. The Stravinskyian ballet—or, one should say, the Stravinsky-Balanchine ballet—is characterized by the development of equal, abstract closed forms of movement and sound which in no way intersect or "express" each other but remain completely independent if parallel.

In addition to his ballets, however, Stravinsky also created a unique and important music theatre built on closed forms and on abstraction—one would almost say ritualization—of content. Interestingly enough, while the forms remain closed, the materials are open and various. Thus, *Renard* uses an on-stage chamber orchestra, motionless singers and actor-mimes; *L'Histoire du soldat* replaces the singing with narration and dialogue and adds dance. *Les Noces* uses an orchestra of percussion and pianos with solo and choral singing and dance-mime. *Oedipus Rex*—designated an "opera-oratorio" and often staged today—uses a narrator, orchestra, chorus, and soloists and is realized scenically in a series of masked marmoreal stage tableaux. *Perséphone* and the more recent, unsuccessful television work, *The Flood* (1962), similarly combine a variety of techniques. Stravinsky has also written three operas that use scene, singing, and stage action in the more-or-less usual way: *Le Rossignol*, an early work in the Russian-French manner (begun in 1909 but only finished after *Le Sacre*), *Mavra*, a one-act burlesque not far removed in manner from *L'Histoire* and *Renard*, and *The Rake's Progress* (1951), Stravinsky's farewell to opera and his final and most complete homage to classical form. In all of these works—after *Le Rossignol*, at least—Stravinsky abstracts the essence of an experience and the essence of a form, and in this process of abstraction he created perhaps the only new and workable musico-dramatic form of the first half-century. The importance of the Stravinskyian mixed-genre theatre has perhaps been underestimated; the mixing of means in the context of schematic, prototypical, neo-classical forms, the abstraction of classical themes—musical and literary-dramatic—and the treatment of theatrical experience as a kind of ritual embody conceptions of modern musical theatre which remain vital.

Some of the more superficial aspects of Stravinsky's theatrical conceptions—or perhaps parallel and contemporary ideas of similar value—had an immediate and important effect: simplification of treatment and reprise of tonal techniques; use of limited and practical means; stylized treatment of popular subject-matter; clear, closed forms. Exactly like *L'Histoire*, Honegger's *Le Roi David* was written in small, closed forms on a "popular" or folkish text originally for a small Swiss travelling theatrical company; only later was it amplified to its present orchestral form. Milhaud's

Les Chóephores, based on Aeschylus, and his tiny *opéras minutes* are highly stylized treatments of classical subjects. The Poulenc operas—the farce *Les Mamelles de Tirésias,* Cocteau's monodrama *La Voix Humaine,* and the rather grand and impressive *Dialogues des Carmélites*—use clear, fastidious tonal techniques in contexts of great simplicity and directness. The clearest representative of Stravinskyian techniques on the modern stage, however, is Carl Orff, whose musico-theatrical style is based on tonal simplicity and directness carried to an extreme point. Works like *Carmina Burana* (a Stravinskyian type of scenic-dance-oratorio) and its companions *Catulli Carmina* and *Il Trionfo di Afrodite* are vast expansions of one small part of the Stravinskyian esthetic—stylistic abstractions from *Les Noces* expanded to fill up an entire musical *Weltanschauung.* The later operatic works, such as *Der Mond, Die Kluge,* and *Antigonae,* are conceived more completely in terms of dramatic planes and juxtapositions. In *Antigonae* a huge percussion apparatus punctuates music of chant and intonation. Ostinato and rhythmic outburst are set against simple melodic curves, the whole structured in immobile blocks and layers.

The sheer size of the physical apparatus of nineteenth-century opera inevitably provoked a reaction in the twentieth century; the new simplicity and the new concision of form and expression were also accompanied by an enormous reduction of means and scope. Strauss, of all people, was an important pioneer here, although his *Ariadne auf Naxos,* scored for an orchestra of twenty-three musicians, now generally appears in the context of "grand opera." Works like *L'Histoire, Mavra,* and *Renard* actually established a new genre of short chamber opera that was both practical and appealing. Hindemith (who, in *Wir bauen eine Stadt* of 1930, wrote a tiny "opera" for performance by young children) composed several chamber operas in the 1920's—notably *Neues vom Tage* and *Hin und Zurück*—with brief, lively, contemporary subjects and musical matter. Kurt Weill's early operas are similar—short, bustling, concise and small-scaled, freely diatonic and tonal in a serious, lively, contrapuntal way. Only later and under the influence of Brecht did Weill definitively turn to popular forms. Like Stravinsky, Weill wanted to re-create the "number" opera concept, but in the context of a meaningful musical play filled with the popular music of the cabaret. With Weill, the divergent streams —divergent since the nineteenth-century division between popular musical theatre and opera—merge again in a musical theatre of social consciousness.

The intense and brilliant irony of Brecht's stage conceptions—a kind of aftermath of "expressionism" turned to the purposes of satire and devastating social commentary—combined with Weill's gift for writing a brilliant, bitter, low-down, dead-pan cabaret melody framed in a kind of intentionally brutal and awkward rhythmic-instrumental setting, obtained an enormous success for these works and they continue to hold the stage. But the "new" musical theatre of social concern has proved to be of very limited application. Interrupted by the Nazi period and the war, the Weill-Brecht type has had serious consequences only in East

Germany (Hanns Eisler, 1898–1962; Paul Dessau, b. 1894) where Brecht remained active till his death, and in the United States, where Weill took refuge during the war. Weill himself became active in American musical theatre, and works like *Street Scene, Knickerbocker Holiday*, and *Lady in the Dark* had a strong influence on the development of the modern musical theatre of Rodgers and Hammerstein, and of Lerner and Loewe. Similarly, the concept of a serious popular theatre built on contemporary themes of social significance, using popular and accessible musical and theatrical means, was passed on by Weill directly to Marc Blitzstein (*The Cradle Will Rock, No for an Answer, Regina*) and to Leonard Bernstein (*Wonderful Town, Candide, West Side Story*—whose prototype is, recognizably, *Street Scene*).

Besides the popular musical theatre and its more-or-less serious adaptations—we can include here the naïve sophistication of the unique and isolated *Porgy and Bess* and the sophisticated simplicity of the Thomson-Stein operas, *Four Saints in Three Acts* and *The Mother of Us All*—there are a few notable examples of serious, "grand" opera in English, most of them by Benjamin Britten. In works like *Peter Grimes, The Rape of Lucretia, The Turn of the Screw*, and *A Midsummer Night's Dream*, Britten has succeeded in renovating operatic tradition in terms of the English language. With the exception of certain special, non-traditional works like *Noye's Fludde*, Britten's stage music adapts itself quite naturally to the conventional operatic structures.

On the other hand, a whole series of related American operas, heavily dependent on Menotti and Italian "verismo" tradition, are suffocated by the past (their dominant theme is often nostalgia or regret). At the other extreme are the many avant-garde manifestations which employ or do not employ vocal and/or other sounds in the context of some kind of theatrical experience but which submerge the generating role of sound much more thoroughly than, say, the recitative operas of Peri and which —unless one accepts the sociological significance of the "happening" and related activities—appear as ideas without, as yet, notable consequences. Until the present moment, contemporary musical theatre is still dominated by Broadway and by the attractive small genre of near-Broadway, near-popular, or near-folk opera that begins with *Porgy and Bess* and *Street Scene* and seems to approach a dead end in works like Douglas Moore's *The Ballad of Baby Doe* and the musical theatre of Leonard Bernstein. The moment for something new is perhaps ripe.

Bibliography

Probably the best book in English on Puccini is Mosco Carner's (London, 1958). Norman Del Mar's Strauss project has been mentioned above, as has the Mitchell-Keller book on Britten; the October–November, 1952, issue of *Musical*

Opinion (London) was devoted to "Britten, Strauss, and the Future of Opera." Joseph Kerman's *Opera as Drama* (New York, 1956) is a general essay which includes contemporary problems; but there is surprisingly little material of note anywhere on opera and musical theater as popular forms—Menotti and neo-verismo, Kurt Weill, Blitzstein and Bernstein, the Broadway musical and the off-Broadway Brechtian show. The only musical publication to cover musical theatre in all of its aspects over a period of years was the American magazine *Modern Music* in the years of its existence, 1926–1946 (see the author's article in *Perspectives of New Music* already cited; see also the magazine itself *passim*). There is a collection of essays on *Stravinsky in the Theatre* (ed. Minna Lederman, New York, 1949). The program of the 1964 Maggio Musicale Fiorentino, which was devoted to "expressionism," contains a number of studies (in Italian) concerning "expressionist theatre." George Perle has published several articles on Alban Berg's *Wozzeck* and *Lulu* (see the Columbia University *Music Forum*, v. 1, 1966; *Journal of the American Musicological Society*, Summer, 1964; *Music Review*, November, 1965; etc.) and is working on a major study of these operas.

PART FOUR

Atonality
and
Twelve-tone
Music

IO

The Viennese School

Schoenberg and the twelve-tone idea

After *Pierrot Lunaire*, Op. 21 (1912), and the *Four Orchestral Songs*, Op. 22 (1914–1915), both written on the eve of World War I, no new work of Schoenberg appeared for almost ten years, although for part of that time he worked on a large oratorio, *Die Jacobsleiter*. All of the composers who participated in the revolutions of the first twelve or fifteen years of the century moved afterwards toward some kind of artistic, expressive, and/or intellectual synthesis of the new materials in new but clear and comprehensive forms; Schoenberg, whose atonal works of 1910–1915 represent the most thorough-going renovation and extension of the musical material, proposed the most radical and thorough consolidation. In *Die Jacobsleiter* he worked his way towards a systematic exploitation of the complete gamut of tempered chromatic sounds. The oratorio was never completed—perhaps because Schoenberg discovered the basic conception only through the art of composition and each step forward seemed to imply the recasting of what had come before. But the Piano Pieces, Op. 23, and the *Serenade*, Op. 24 (both completed in 1923), contain twelve-tone music; and the Piano Suite, Op. 25 (1921–1923), and Wind Quintet, Op. 26 (1924), are complete twelve-tone conceptions from start of finish.[1]

Schoenberg's twelve-tone procedure is a synthesis of two formal ideas which are actually separable and which have in fact been used independently; both ideas appear in embryo—not necessarily connected, and more or less informally—in the "atonal" music of Schoenberg himself, and of Berg and Webern. The first is the continuous use of patterns which contain all of the twelve pitches; the second is the organization of pitch materials according to a consistent order principle. Thus, in Schoenberg's "classical" formulation of the technique, each piece is based on a given ordering of the twelve tempered pitches—abstracted (without regard for octave or register) as the twelve-tone series or row[2]—and the work itself is an exposition or realization of this order structure. Schoenberg thought of musical space as multi-dimensional and he regarded this space as having essential unity. Thus, any given pattern of notes—and, specifically, a series of twelve different pitches—can appear unbroken and without internal change (like a physical object being rotated in space) in four forms: forward, backward, upside-down, and upside-down backward. Here is the abstracted form of the twelve-tone series of Schoenberg's *Piano Piece*, Op. 33 (1928), in its four forms—known technically as the original, retrograde, inversion, and retrograde-inversion (Example 10-1). Each of these forms may, of course, be transposed to any of the other eleven degrees of the chromatic scale (in Example 10-1, the inversion is shown at the fifth—I-5 —level); in all cases, the internal relationships—the intervals—remain constant and all twelve notes appear once and only once.

The question of the repetition of tones in twelve-tone music is much misunderstood. Clearly, in the underlying ordering, each class of pitches (regardless of octave) can appear once and only once if all twelve pitches are to be always represented. In the actual compositional realization, however, small repetitions of notes or groups of notes often appear without disrupting the larger cycles of twelve notes. Furthermore, since the twelve-note groupings may appear as purely melodic voices in counterpoint (each line made up of constantly revolving cycles of the basic row), or as blocks of chords (i.e., three chords of four notes each, four chords of three notes,

---

[1] Apparently Schoenberg first formulated his twelve-tone ideas in precise form in 1921. It is not clear whether the last piece of Op. 23 or the first of Op. 25 was the first actual twelve-tone composition.

[2] The terms "series" and "row" (hence "serial" and "row" music) are used interchangeably. Milton Babbitt has proposed the mathematical term "set." Twelve-tone (or "twelve-note") music is sometimes called dodecaphony, the adjectival form of which is dodecaphonic.

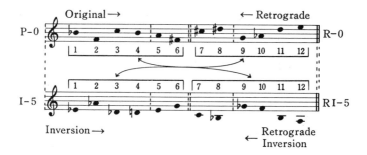

EXAMPLE 10-1. Schoenberg, *Piano Piece*, Op. 33a.

a. The row, in all the forms used in the suite.

b. Präludium, beginning.

c. Gavotte, beginning.

EXAMPLE 10-2. Schoenberg, *Piano Suite*, Op. 25. Quoted by permission of Mrs. Gertrud Schoenberg and Universal Edition.

d. Musette, beginning.

e. Intermezzo, beginning.

f. Menuett, beginning.

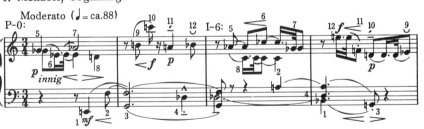

g. Gigue, beginning.

EXAMPLE 10-2 continued.

Portrait of Arnold Schoenberg by Oskar Kokoschka. Reproduced by permission of Annie Knize.

etc.), or as some combination of the above, certain duplications may appear between parts; this, however, can also be avoided by distributing the twelve notes between the melodic and harmonic parts or by conceiving the music in aggregates of sound in such a way that the complete twelve-note groupings constantly succeed each other in small time segments. All of these questions are, in the end, compositional matters; they do not necessarily disturb the basic "twelve-toneness" of the conception.

a. First subject.

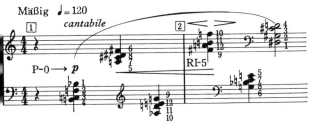

b. Second subject.

EXAMPLE 10-3. Schoenberg, *Piano Piece*, Op. 33a. Quoted by permission of Mrs. Gertrud Schoenberg and Universal Edition.

Schoenberg's first tendency was to use the row melodically and contrapuntally, a technique which produces a kind of on-going variational form.[3] Later, a desire to integrate the harmonic character of the music directly with the row led him to conceive of the row in chordal groupings out of which new and significant melodic elements might appear. Here is the way the twelve-tone material of the *Piano Suite*, Op. 25, is realized compositionally at the beginning of the various movements (Example 10-2); the principle is obviously that of the variation-suite. In the *Piano Piece*, Op. 33a, however, the original presentation is chordal; the basic units are the three four-note chords at the beginning and they color the entire work; only later, as the piece develops and unfolds, are lines extracted (Example 10-3). Note the close relationship between the phrasing and structural articulation of the piece and the twelve-tone groupings; this kind of phrasing is particularly clear at the start and at the main points of articulation in the piece. The first three chords present a harmonic ar-

---

[3] The variational principle is perhaps the oldest and most basic formal device in music; it is certainly not associated—as "Sonata form" was—uniquely with tonality. Nevertheless, variational principles do not play an important role in early twentieth-century music and began being re-introduced only in the context of the new synthesis.

rangement of the original form of the row; the second three, the retrograde inversion. In the next three measures, the arrangement takes the form of a succession of pitches with one form of the row (the retrograde inversion) in the upper register, and another (the retrograde) in the lower parts; measures 6 and 7, however, develop the pitch material of measures 1 and 2 in the original order. The following measures again present different forms of the material in "contrapuntal juxtapositions"; notice the important use of repetition as an extension device in measures 8 and 9 and in the new section beginning at measure 14. If the independent use of registers is kept in mind, it is not difficult to follow the twelve-tone thread through measure 20. In measure 20, however, the first "irregularity" occurs: the final two notes of both the retrograde and the retrograde inversion do not appear; instead the music seems to reverse its steps so that the return at measure 21 to the outline shape of measure 14 begins at the middle point of the rows. It is clear that from measure 14 onwards (see Example 10-3b), the basic arrangement of the row material is no longer in three groups of fours but in two groups of sixes (subdivided into smaller units of threes). If the given rows are examined, it will be seen that the collection of the first six pitches of the original contains the same notes (although in a different order) as the first six pitches of the retrograde inversion; and, of course, the same is true of the last six pitches of each form. Thus, if the original is presented simultaneously with its inversion (at the given transposition), the first and last six notes of each form combine to produce new, complete twelve-tone combinations; this remarkable fact, carefully calculated by Schoenberg, provides the structural basis for the music as it evolves from four-note chord sounds towards the arrangements in six-note groupings. Beginning at the end of measure 27, there is a kind of development section (continuing the development that began in measures 21 and 22) in which the pairs of three-note groupings began to appear transposed onto different levels (up a step and then down a fourth, first presented in complementary six-note groups and in complete transposed rows). The re-establishment of the original row material at the original levels after the *fermata* in measure 32, the return to the conditions of measure 14 in measure 35, the unified arrangement of complete rows in short descending and ascending phrases in measures 37 and 38, and the final re-interpretation of measures 1 and 2 at the end can be easily traced.[4] The mere counting of the notes of the row is in itself meaningless without a clear understanding of the way in which the sound of the resulting harmonic and melodic combinations penetrates the entire piece; the way in which the parts intersect and relate forward and backward; the role of repetition, of changing register, of accent, and of dynamic in de-

---

[4] The attentive score-reader—perhaps even the alert listener—will find, in addition to the above-mentioned omissions at measure 20, a note taken from the lower register and substituted for a missing note in the upper in measure 22, exchanges of note order in measures 29 and 37, and a clear misprint in measure 35.

fining the phrase structure, which in itself is intimately related to the twelve-tone process; the way in which the piece moves from one type of structure and organization to another—from a static idea to a developmental one—and then back again. The twelve-tone technique is not a form imposed from the outside, it *is* the piece; that is, it is the way the ideas of the piece take shape in time—at once, the content and the form.

A great deal of discussion has centered on the precise definition of the role that the twelve-tone idea should and does play in musical composition. Schoenberg himself rejected the term "system"; others have shown that the twelve-tone principle does in itself form a "system" in a precise sense. Schoenberg preferred the word "method," in the sense of procedure, although in his actual composition it probably functioned more as a mode of musical thinking analogous in certain ways to tonality. The twelve-tone principle was, for him, a way of organizing musical thought that is coherent, that controls every aspect of every piece but is uniquely established anew by each piece, and that can generate appropriate and organic forms by relating every aspect of a piece to an overall and underlying conception. The mere arrangements of the row in a piece do not constitute the whole piece anymore than the E–flat tonality of Beethoven's Third Symphony equals the whole "Eroica";[5] but the twelve-tone conception in a Schoenberg piece—like the tonal conception in Beethoven—pervades the whole, gives it its characteristic sonorous and intellectual qualities, and permits the composer to express his ideas through the means of a big, coherent, and organic form. To say that is to say a great deal. Schoenberg was perhaps the true classicist among contemporary composers because he understood the underlying principles of classical form and discovered a viable equivalent in modern terms.

Schoenberg set about establishing the universality and scope of his new art immediately. With the exception of the choruses of Op. 27 and 28, all of the early twelve-tone compositions are pieces of considerable size which evoke their classical equivalents not simply by references or parallels in texture, rhythm, or form, but because they also embody a unity of thought and expression in terms of large-scale statement, process, and resolution. Thus, in a multi-movement work like the Piano Suite, Op. 25, or the Septet, Op. 29 (1926), the basic material is realized in a series of different guises, each revealing aspects of the underlying idea, each with its own possibilities of discovery, elucidation, and expression. In the Wind Quintet, Op. 26, and the Third String Quartet, Op. 30 (1927), the twelve-tone ideas become subjects for development. The row—or significant segments from it—generates very specific shapes which, in turn, develop and interrelate over wide time–spans to make long and expressive structures formed, for the most part, at the very outer limits of performer and listener capabilities. (A work like the Wind Quintet has not yet been

---

[5] The usual spelling-out of the row and row-forms in analyses and discussions is to be considered only a helpful abstraction, valid only as far as it is useful.

properly realized in performance, although that moment will undoubtedly come soon enough now.) The row itself does not really function as a theme nor, certainly, as a scale or mode (as it does sometimes in Berg's music), but as a set of materials, a complex of relationships, offering enormous possibilities to the ordered imagination that can master them. Schoenberg was able to rediscover organic large form—classical by analogy only, and not, in spite of the analogies, "neo-classical" at all; in Schoenberg's mature, large-scaled works, the big form is an essential and inevitable result of the working-out of the implications of a rich basic material.

At the end of the 1920's and specifically with the *Variations for Orchestra*, Op. 31, of 1928, Schoenberg centered his concern on the direct derivation of a form out of the implications of the basic material. Although the general plan of the Variations is traditional (introduction, theme, variations, coda), the conception of these variations is both universal and yet utterly specific and unique to the work. The variations themselves grow out of the conflict between the generality of the basic material (the intervals and relationships which appear in the introduction in fragmented, unordered form) and its very specific realization as a row-theme. The two very different conceptions of the row—on the one hand, as generative material far beneath the surface (functioning, as Schoenberg believed, in a manner somewhat analogous to tonality and not necessarily consciously perceived) and on the other, as thematic material—are here very deliberately juxtaposed; this is, so to speak, the dialectic of the piece. With each new variation-transformation, the thematic character of the row becomes again more and more generalized until, in the long and remarkable finale, virtually a new formal level is reached; in this finale, the idea of transformation has been taken up into an on-going twelve-tone structure. The theme, as it were, is absorbed into the row idea which generated it in the first place. Thus, the work moves from the specific towards the universal, from musical idea towards structure, from "inspiration" towards intellectual resolution.

In *Von Heute auf Morgen*, Schoenberg's Op. 32 (1928), and in the opera *Moses und Aron*, the completed portion of which was written in the following few years, the twelve-tone method was applied, apparently for the first time, to music for the theatre. *Von Heute auf Morgen* treats a light, contemporary subject. *Moses und Aron* has a rather lofty philosophical text by Schoenberg himself, full of intellectual oppositions and dualisms, which are reflected in the music itself. One curious thing about *Moses und Aron* is that although only two acts were set—the brief third act remains only in text—the existing music is complete in thought and structure; the work is a unity which generates a richness and diversity of ideas and means: huge divided singing-and-*Sprechstimme* choruses; the solo voice of Aron and the spoken part of Moses; a large and masterfully handled orchestra with a wide range of colors. The opposition between rich, even sensual variety and color on the one hand and a complex intellectual unity on the other[6] is a direct image of the philosophical issues which animate the text.

The forms of the *Accompaniment to a Film Scene*, Op. 34 (1929–1930), are also presumably dramatic, but this *Begleitungsmusik* was written for an imaginary cinema; the events of the scene are purely internal musical events, and the "dramatic" form is nothing but an expressive function of the ideas and the material.

In 1933, after the advent of Hitler, Schoenberg was forced to leave Germany. In the same year, he came to the United States, where he remained for the rest of his life—principally in California, where he taught at the University of California at Los Angeles. A number of his American works show a marked or partial return to a tonal idiom: a Suite for string orchestra (1934), a *Theme and Variations* for band (Op. 43, 1943), and the *Variations on a Recitative* for organ (Op. 40, 1941) are practical pieces, almost *Gebrauchsmusik;* and works like the *Ode to Napoleon* of 1942 and *A Survivor from Warsaw* of 1947 use tonal references in tension with twelve-tone techniques. On the other hand, the Fourth String Quartet (1936) and the Violin and Piano Concertos (1934–1936 and 1942) are large-scale, thematic, wholly twelve-tone structures in which the technique becomes fluent and pliable, focused in a way that parallels the role played by tonality in similar classical forms.

Schoenberg's attitude towards this material in no way implies a return from or a renunciation of his early ideas; quite the contrary, it suggests rather a widening of the possibilities of the technique. In certain early works of Schoenberg and other twelve-tone composers there is a conscious attempt to avoid any combination of tones which might suggest a tonal superseded or bypassed. (The reasons for banning, say, a major triad in reference or center. Later on, this rather arbitrary rule-of-thumb was a twelve-tone piece are, presumably, psychological rather than musical, and, in fact, there are some very successful twelve-tone pieces built largely on triads; e.g. the Webern String Quartet.) Schoenberg expanded his conception of the possibilities of twelve-tone technique enormously in the later part of his life, and very late works like the String Trio, Op. 45 (1946), and the *Phantasy* for violin and piano, Op. 47 (1949), evolve distinctive new forms out of new material. Schoenberg came to think of the row material, not as a specifically linear ordering but as a series of groupings of pitches and intervals whose potentialities would be revealed by the process of the piece. In the Trio, for example, the character of the groupings is revealed only gradually (Example 10-4). Thus in the first measure there is a total chromatic material divided into two groups of six notes, the distinctive feature being the half step trill. In the second

---

[6] Musically resolved in the existing two acts; hence the impossibility of music for the third, which was to demonstrate the triumph of the latter over the former.

EXAMPLE 10-4. Schoenberg, *String Trio*, Op. 45. Quoted by permission of Mrs. Gertrud Schoenberg and Universal Edition.

EXAMPLE 10-4 continued.

measure, the pitch content of these groupings is established: B-C-G–sharp-F–sharp-G-F for one "hexachord"; the inversion (transposed) produces the other six notes. A primary order form of this material is revealed only in the fifth measure, first in groups of two notes divided between the violin and viola, then in a strictly linear form in the viola (accompanied by harmonies made up of complementary forms of the same material transposed to fill out the twelve-note groupings). In measures 6 and 7, the same material reappears now in four-note groupings. In measures 8–13, there is a systematic presentation of the material in three complete rows—taking off from the basic form of measure 4—out of which the violin extracts a new line which in itself is a new grouping of twelve-tones.[7] These techniques, which bind harmonic and linear ideas closely together with timbre, dynamic, rhythm, and phrase, provide a remarkable sense of continuity and even inevitability within a musical material which is constantly changing, constantly in motion yet always basically the same. This kind of linking technique—a kind of continuous development—suggests the possibilities of strict forms which are nevertheless open at the far end, forms in which everything is intertwined and in which the motion from one sound to another, from one end of the piece to the other, seems inevitable yet remains, until it is actually realized, unforeseen.

Schoenberg's music, unlike that of his pupils Berg and Webern, has never been popular and it probably never will be. All his life Schoenberg faced obstinate incomprehension on the part of musicians and the public, but probably the deepest and most ironic challenge his work has yet had to face is that of the younger European avant-gardists who have posthumously charged him with having failed to realize the consequences of his own revolution, of having remained a classicist all his life faithful to the traditional notions of what constitutes a piece of music, of having failed to extend the concept of serial technique beyond the organization of the twelve tempered chromatic pitches. There is a grain of half-truth in the charge: Schoenberg was, in a deep sense, a classicist, and of all the great early contemporaries, the one most involved in re-discovering the

[7] Later in the work, secondary row material is formed by permutations within the "hexachords"; the pitch content of the hexachords, however, remains constant.

deepest and most universal significance of the great tradition. But it is not accurate to imply that he was not sensitive to the implications of what he was doing; the only valid test is one which examines realizations in terms of premises—overt and implied. The criticism, in any case, completely overlooks both the early and the late works with all their continuing significance even for the most recent kind of creative problems. Even beyond this, the charge is a purely polemical one in that it criticizes Schoenberg for not having had a set of different premises; it has the same order of relevance as would a criticism of Einstein that charged him with having failed to realize the consequences of his own revolution by virtue of his having remained faithful all his life to some notion of classical determinism. It is true that, in a sense, Schoenberg wrote cause-and-effect music and that John Cage and even Karlheinz Stockhausen do not. But Einstein's physics is hardly that of Newton, and cause and effect in Schoenberg is scarcely what it was in Rameau.

Just as Schoenberg was the first to discover and explore a rich and complex new sonorous universe, he was the first to discover valid laws which operate in that universe. The parallel with scientific inquiry would have pleased Schoenberg, although he himself came out of the rather more dubiously "scientific" tradition of Hegel and historical determinism—he thought of himself as having, like Hegel or Marx, discovered immutable laws about the process of history which made his conquest of total chromaticism and his twelve-tone procedure a historical necessity. But it is not necessary to accept the analogy between the process of inquiry and discovery on the one hand and that of creation on the other (although the analogy has, interestingly enough, been recognized in many recent studies of the philosophy and psychology of scientific inquiry). Schoenberg's early music is the fruit of what we might call analytic inquiry: the refusal to accept traditional hypotheses; the discovery of a whole new set of realities; the creative exploration of the artistic, intellectual, and psychological significance of these new realities, "tested" in creative terms in a series of works of art. His later music is, in the best sense, synthetic: the statement of new unifying hypotheses which relate these realities in terms of a creative synthesis to underlying artistic, psychological, and intellectual truths. As we shall see, these processes have been recapitulated in avant-garde thought since World War II.

Berg and Webern

Schoenberg's influence on Berg was, in one sense, decisive, yet Berg never took from Schoenberg any more than he needed to realize his own ideas. Thus, although Berg's later work is impossible to imagine without the influence of the twelve-tone idea, he never wrote a really thoroughgoing twelve-tone work. His *Chamber Concerto* for violin and piano with thirteen instruments (1923–1925) is not twelve-tone at all; it is, to be sure, full of complicated numerical patterns, but these are of a type typical of Berg, not of Schoenberg. The influence of Schoenberg is discernible in the complex and rich web of structural relationships derived from the initial statement of the material—not a twelve-tone row but a three-part subject based on those letters in the names "Schoenberg," "Berg," and "Webern" which have musical equivalents. Out of this unpromising and arbitrary material, Berg creates a big three-movement structure: a concerto movement with piano solo, one for violin solo, and a finale for both soloists. Like many of Berg's works, the Concerto tries to be inclusive; it is long and full of a great variety of ideas, materials, and techniques. The big shape of the piece emerges—not without problems which present formidable obstacles to the performers—from the free, disassociated character of Berg's imagination and the conscious restraints of form and technique which he imposed on himself with an almost mystical fervor.

The *Lyric Suite* for string quartet (1925–1926) is, in its individual movements at least, less ambitious, but by turning his imaginative enterprise to a series of shorter, characteristic movements Berg was able to create expressive structures that grow naturally out of the ideas themselves. The ideas of these movements are not merely themes in the traditional sense but also colors and expressive shapes, an aspect which Berg emphasizes by qualifying the tempo indications with strong, associative "color" words: *Allegro giovale, Largo desolato, Presto delirando, Trio estatico,* and so forth. Two of the movements are twelve-tone, but even here Berg uses the technique not so much as a structural principle but as a way to "color" the music from the inside. Thus, the famous *Allegro misterioso* is the most elaborately twelve-tone movement Berg ever wrote, but all the careful, precise manipulations on the printed page are no more (and, to be sure, no less) than a great whispering, rustling, rushing murmur.

The concert aria *Der Wein,* after poetry by Baudelaire (1929), is Berg's first and only attempt at writing a large concert work completely unified in row technique, but even here the function of the row is special and peculiarly Bergian. The series, which begins with an ascending D-minor scale, works not so much as a theme nor, on the other hand, as underpinning but much more simply: as a kind of mode in the old, original meaning of that term. The ancient modes—or, for example, the Indian *raga*—are not "scales" or "tonalities" in the modern sense but repertoires of melodic formulas, often associated with specific kinds of rhythmic ideas, embellishments, and tone colors. Thus, an Indian *raga* is not a theme, and there may be no definitive, meaningful way of writing it down as a "scale"; but a piece is instantly recognizable as being "in" a certain *raga* by its characteristic turns of phrase. Berg used the twelve-tone row in just this way (so did Schoenberg, but secondarily). In the opera *Lulu* this becomes the basis of a rich and complex technique of dramatic and psychological identification.

The text of *Lulu* (1928–1934) was drawn by Berg himself from two plays of Franz Wedekind; the opera was finished in short-score form, but part of the orchestration of the last act was left incomplete by the composer at his death and the work is known today in a makeshift form consisting of the first two acts and the final scene of the third. This is exceptionally unfortunate because, as George Perle has pointed out, *Lulu* has Berg's typically symmetrical form with the third act providing dramatic climax, psychological realization, a good deal of the intellectual meaning, and musical recapitulation and resolution. Lulu herself is a kind of archetypical character, part whore, part Earth-mother; and as an incarnation of female sexuality she moves with the sublime inevitability and indifference of Nature through a series of love adventures that are in turn macabre, tragic, comic, grotesque, and sublime. Berg's music is at once specific (it defines the characters by their rows, by the way they sing, even by the orchestral sounds that dog their footsteps) and general (in the way it universalizes a macabre piece of grotesque irony into a grand tragi-comedy).

Berg's last completed work was his Violin Concerto (1935), commissioned by the American violinist Louis Krasner; the work, dedicated to the memory of Manon Gropius (the daughter of the architect and Alma Mahler, who was also Berg's patron), became Berg's own monument. The two-movement concerto has a row which consists of a series of interlocking major and minor triads with a whole-tone tetrachord at the end. (Example 10-5a). This does function in Schoenberg's twelve-tone sense to a considerable degree, but its basic significance comes out of its use—as described above—as an underlying, unifying point of reference which enables Berg to pull together a whole variety of seemingly unrelated and disparate ideas: perfect fifths suggested by the open strings of the violin (Example 10-5b); a triadic, quasi-tonal harmonic structure (Example 10-5c); "Viennese waltz"-like themes quite strictly derived from the row (Example 10-5d); a Carinthian folksong (Example 10-5e); and a Bach chorale (Example 10-5f). The intensity and diversity of Berg's ideas come close to shattering their very structure; it is almost as if he wanted to charge his music with more expressive weight than it could bear. But the very range of expression, combined with the carefully defined freedom of technique, makes him much less of a traditionalist than he has sometimes been made out to be. Berg's obvious references to the past are no more a good model for a new music today than his specific musical personality is a good subject for imitation; but his work remains meaningful because he was able to communicate precise, predetermined, expressive forms which somehow seem to grow out of the wide scope of his creative imagination.

During and after World War I, Webern was occupied with a series of eight consecutive vocal sets, mostly for solo voice and instruments; among these are the Opus 17 songs (1924), Webern's first twelve-tone works. Webern accepted Schoenberg's ideas neither casually nor quickly; but with the String Trio, Op. 20, of 1927, the Symphony, Op. 21, of the

a. The row.

b. Solo violin, Introduction to First Movement.

c. Principal subject, Andante, First Movement.

d. "Viennese" themes, Allegretto, First Movement.

e. Carinthian Folksong, Allegretto, First Movement.

EXAMPLE 10-5. Berg, *Violin Concerto*. Quoted by permission of Universal Edition.

f. Bach chorale, Adagio, Second Movement.

EXAMPLE 10-5 continued.

following year, and the Quartet for violin, clarinet, tenor saxophone, and
piano, Op. 22, of 1930, he embraced the strictest kind of twelve-tone procedure and fully incorporated this into his own esthetic. The twelve-tone
row of the Concerto, Op. 24 (1934), for nine instruments is shown in
Example 10-6a. The basic intervallic units are the same as those of the
Bagatelle mentioned above: the major third and the minor second. The
row itself further breaks down into four groups of three notes, the last
three of which are transpositions of the other forms of the original—
retrograde inversion, retrograde, inversion; also the retrograde inversion
of the whole row at the given transposition preserves the pitch identities
of the three-note groups. Here are a few measures of the realization of
this concept (Example 10-6b). The actual structure of the row is crucial;
in the second movement, for instance (Example 10-6c), the groups of
threes are formed by single tones in the "melodic" instruments comple-
mented by two-note harmonic groupings in the piano. The solo line
consists of the initial notes of each three-note group of the row, which themselves form other transpositions of the identical three-note group. The
interlocking of these groupings is carried out systematically. Transpositions of this material are chosen which produce further relations and
further identities. Certain pitches and certain groups of two and three
notes reappear in different forms and transpositions of the row material,
and these relationships are exploited in terms of register, tone color, position in the phrase, and so forth; non-pitch aspects of the music are thus
brought into close relationship with the twelve-tone material.

From one point of view, Webern's solutions are classical: classical
tonal music also had this one-to-one relationship between all aspects of
the musical material—or, at any rate, between pitch, rhythm, and the
dynamic shape of the phrases—and Webern's periods are indeed classical
in a strict sense. The first movement of the Symphony is a rather closely
worked (and somewhat arbitrary) sonata form with an exposition (ending
with the traditional double-bar) and a careful recapitulation; many of

Webern's later works are sets of variations based on a kind of "song form" phrase structure with real antecedent and consequent phrases. Webern's tendency to transform and re-create certain aspects of the classical tradition is particularly evident in his twelve-tone instrumental works, which are, in many ways, much less far-reaching and much more classically abstract than his earlier "atonal" pieces; to the works mentioned above, can be added the *Variations for Piano*, Op. 27 (1936), the String Quartet, Op. 28 (1938), and the *Variations for Orchestra*, Op. 30 (1940). On the other hand, in the later vocal works, and most particularly in *Das Augenlicht*, Op. 26 (1935), and the two cantatas, Op. 29 and 31 (1939, 1941–1943), the verbal material and the relationships between solo, choral, and instrumental sound at once seem to suggest a whole new set of problems

a. The row.

b. First movement, meas. 1-5.

c. Second movement, meas. 1-18.

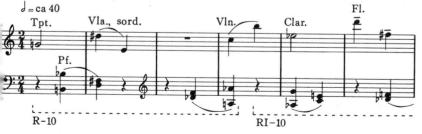

EXAMPLE 10-6. Webern, *Concerto for Nine Instruments*, Op. 24. Quoted by permission of Universal Edition.

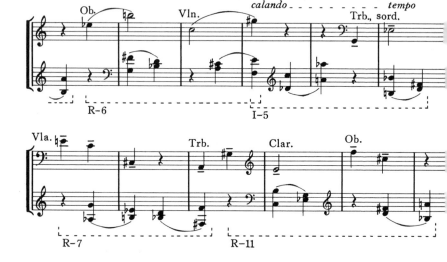

EXAMPLE 10-6 continued.

and solutions. The conceptions of line and of the relationships between line and harmonic structure are new and generate new ideas of organizing expressive musical thoughts; indeed, the very obliteration of the classical distinction between line and harmony (and, indeed, to some extent between pitch, duration, timbre, and intensity), characteristic of the early works of Webern and Schoenberg and later schematized by Webern in his earlier twelve-tone works, is again taken up in these later vocal compositions.

Webern extended serial principles into many musical domains and in such a way as to make his miniature forms a function of the ideas themselves. The superficial influence of Webern was the esthetic of silence and brevity; more profound ideas grew out of the organic qualities of his thinking, almost totally detached from the notion of on-going process, the music implied from the start by its own premises, yet unforeseen. In spite of the complex implications of Webern's work, its most immediate qualities are clarity and transparency of idea realized within tiny, utterly schematic and crystalline forms. These qualities are also, and in spite of appearances, personable and inimitable. The long-range significance of Webern's work may turn out to be, not so much the isolation of the single musical event—the bits of glowing sound set in a starry void—or the consistency and purity of the ideas, but rather the richness of the reconstruction of form. Webern reduced the experience of sound to its essentials; he also demonstrated the possibility of an organic reintegration which evolved from universal prototypes into new and meaningful expressive structures.

Bibliography

The founding fathers produced surprisingly little in the way of theoretical, analytical, or pedagogical twelve-tone formulations. There has been, however, no shortage of texts from the later generations: Josef Rufer, *Composition with Twelve Notes* (New York, 1954); Ernst Křenek, *Studies in Counterpoint* (New York, 1940); Leopold Spinner, *A Short Introduction to the Technique of Twelve-Tone Composition;* Herbert Eimert, *Lehrbuch der Zwölftontechnik* (Wiesbaden, 1950; also translated into Italian). Most of these are prescriptive teaching abstractions which seldom reflect the reality and sometimes actually violate the substance of the music of the Viennese.

There is no generally adequate history of twelve-tone ideas or of the "school." It is now generally agreed that Josef Matthias Hauer's *Zwölftontechnik* (published Vienna, 1926, but developed earlier) and certain early compositions of Nicolay Rosslavetz preceded Schoenberg in showing a twelve-tone formulation. The origins of twelve-tone ideas have been discussed by Eimert; by Willi Reich, in *Alte und neue Musik* (Zürich, 1952); and by Egon Wellesz, *The Origins of Schoenberg's Twelve-Tone System* (Washington, 1958). The best general discussion of the techniques can be found in George Perle's *Serial Composition and Atonality* (Berkeley and Los Angeles, 1963). Schoenberg's writings have been mentioned earlier; they can be supplemented by Rufer's catalogue of Schoenberg's works (London, 1962, from the German original of 1959), which contains many excerpts from unpublished writings of Schoenberg. The author is not aware of any generally satisfactory assessment of Schoenberg which has been published at the time of this writing, although the Schoenberg literature is large and growing. Willi Reich's Berg book, now available in English (see Chapter 4), supplants the often-cited Redlich biography. The transcriptions of Webern's lectures as *The Path to the New Music* have also been mentioned in Chapter 4. An entire issue of *Die Reihe* (No. 2, 1955; tr., Bryn Mawr, Pa., 1958) is devoted to articles on and analyses of Webern; the volume of *Kontrapunkte* mentioned in Chapter 4 (No. 5, Walter Kolneder) contains general information as well as discussions of Opera 1-31. Articles on and analyses of all three of the Viennese can be found in many issues of *Perspectives*, the *Journal of Music Theory*, *The Score*, and *Melos*.

II

The Diffusion of Twelve-tone Music

Between the two wars, the dominant international style was neo-tonal, often specifically "neo-classic" and Stravinskyian. Since World War II and through the last few years, the "neo-classical" idiom has given way to twelve-tone writing of one kind or another. The modern-music world before the war was divided into two bitterly opposed camps: the "neo-classicists" and the "dodecaphonists," Stravinskyians and the Schoenberg followers. The distinction is no longer meaningful: even Stravinsky has been writing twelve-tone music since the 1950's.

The reasons for this shift are complex; it is not helpful to talk of fads, of some mystical superiority of the twelve-tone system, or even of historical necessity. One does not have to accept any dogmatic notions of historical inevitability to recognize that certain ideas have enough innate power and richness to gain—sooner or later—widespread acceptance. One important point is that the twelve-tone idea—in contrast to "neo-classicism"—does not presuppose any particular style. "Neo-classicism" was ultimately a dead end—in spite of its superficial ability to absorb many different kinds of contents—because it is a style or a specific set of styles located in a particular moment of history. So, indeed, are the "styles" of Schoenberg, Berg, and Webern; but the twelve-tone *conception* by no means requires the manner or even the forms employed by its originators. Total chromaticism and the whole range of associated rhythmic, dynamic, and color material offered a rich source of ideas, and the twelve-tone notion of Schoenberg—or some modification of it—suggested a way of handling this material without necessarily dictating a specific idiom. Furthermore—and in spite of Webern's success with small forms—it indicated a way of re-creating large forms, which was hardly possible with most of the neo-tonal, nonfunctional diatonic idioms. Historically the creation of the large form was precisely coincidental with the growth of functional tonality with all its potential for incorporating significant small-range motion and detail into a network of long-range relationships growing out of the tensions and interconnection of horizontal and vertical events and of structural contrasts, extensions, tensions, and resolutions. Many of these big formal tensions are inevitably lost in a non-functional tonal style which tends to build on repetition, juxtaposition, and rhythmic articulation. The rather arbitrary imposition of the skeleton of classical "sonata form" was a stop-gap solution at best. Even some of the most successful neo-tonal structures—works like Stravinsky's *Symphony of Psalms* that go far beyond a mere motion from one tonal area to another—come surprisingly close to serialism. What Schoenberg found was a new way of articulating long-range structures through a rich and suggestive range of musical ideas; and the impact of this was far-reaching. As the characteristic diatonicism of the 1930's began to wane, as the associated esthetic notions of a new simplicity, a new "practicality," and of musical nationalism and populism began to be played out, an increasing number of composers began to concern themselves with chromaticism, with chromatic line and harmony more and more detached from tonal processes. There is a discernible psychological-historical pattern in the gradual aural acceptance of chromatic ideas and processes as "natural"; the pattern is reflected in the cycle of acceptance and influence of this century's major composers, which ran chronologically about like this: Stravinsky and Hindemith, Bartók, Berg, Schoenberg, Webern.

Central Europe

Schoenberg had many pupils besides Berg and Webern but none of

comparable stature. The first important composer outside of the Schoenberg circle to use twelve-tone technique was Ernst Křenek. Křenek, who
was born in Vienna in 1900, was not a Schoenberg pupil and had made
his mark earlier with the opera *Jonny spielt auf*, a lively, dissonant, but
tonal work touched by jazz. In the 1930's, Křenek began using twelve-tone
technique—notably in his big opera, *Karl V*—and, for a number of years,
he alternated or intermingled tonal and twelve-tone ideas. After the war,
Křenek's music became more and more strictly twelve-tone and more and
more concerned with numerological method. A musician of great natural
fluency, Křenek long personified a link between the Hindemith tradition
and that of Schoenberg and Webern; the latest of his long list of compositions similarly link the Schoenberg-Webern tradition with more recent
techniques of serialism.

The accession to power of the Nazis in 1933 and the Austrian *An-
schluss* in 1935 forced Schoenberg to leave Central Europe and abruptly put
an end to the teaching and performance of twelve-tone music. The Nazis—
in the usual totalitarian, ideological fashion—demanded a simple art with a
popular base of support; the new simplicity of composers like Orff and
Egk has remained a powerful anti-twelve-tone force in German-speaking
countries. Nevertheless, after the war, a number of middle-generation
composers—Wolfgang Fortner (b. 1907), Rolf Liebermann (b. 1910),
Boris Blacher (b. 1903)—cautiously adopted some form of dodecaphonic
writing. The French-Swiss composer, Frank Martin (b. 1890), should be
included with this group since a great deal of his work and activity has
been associated with central Europe; his gradual infusion of twelve-tone
techniques into a basically tonal style—mainly for structural strength and
a broadening of scope—is typical.

The break between the older and younger generations in Germany
is very marked. Most of the younger composers—Karlheinz Stockhausen
(b. 1928) is the best-known and most important—actually started their
musical careers as ultra-twelve-tone composers *à la* Webern and developed
from that point. Some of the younger German composers who have become known since the war have continued to develop a twelve-tone idiom
in a fairly direct line of descent from the Viennese; the best-known of
these is Hans Werner Henze (b. 1926), whose work remains closely identified with expressionist techniques: chromatic and twelve-tone in a dis-
sonant-melodic style worked up into large-scale theatrical and symphonic
works. Henze's music represents a conscious attempt to create a free-
flowing, serious, popular-practical twelve-tone style—a latter-day chromatic Hindemith, as it were.

Elsewhere in Europe

Schoenberg had a number of foreign pupils—the Greek Nikos Skalkottas (1904–1949), the Norwegian Farten Valen (1887–1952), the American Adolph Weiss (b. 1891), the Spanish-British composer Roberto Gerhard (b. 1896), and others—who introduced twelve-tone ideas outside of Central Europe, but most of these composers worked in an obscurity only partially dispelled by recent revivals of interest in their work. The first non-Germanic composer to use twelve-tone materials in a distinctive and personal way was Luigi Dallapiccola (b. 1904), an Italian whose only direct relationship with the Viennese was through a brief contact with Webern. Dallapiccola began to write twelve-tone music in the late 1930's under a combined influence of Webern, early Italian lyric tradition, and the so-called "hermetical" movement in contemporary Italian poetry. Later Dallapiccola moved briefly towards a more highly charged, complex style (the opera *Il Prigioniero* of 1944–1948 was influenced by Berg and Schoenberg), but in general, his music represents a distinctive development and extension out of the Webern esthetic—always remembering Webern's strong orientation towards vocal and lyric style. Dallapiccola's twelve-tone technique is generally orthodox and in itself not very complex, but there is a special interest in the way the material is manipulated, much in the manner of a strict counterpoint constructed on given schematic principles or expressive plans: groups of triads, elaborate canonic part-writing, twelve-tone ideas arranged in conjunction with numerical or schematic patterns often of literary or symbolic significance. Dallapiccola has always been oriented towards vocal music and, to a lesser extent, towards the theatre; literary and philosophical notions—derived from Italian "hermetic" poetry and a commitment to the theme of personal and intellectual freedom—have played an important part in his work. Dallapiccola approached twelve-tone technique through the increasing use of chromatic contrapuntal methods based on small serial nuclei (*Tre laudi* of 1936–1937; the *Canti di prigionia* for chorus and percussion orchestra of 1938–1941, one of the composer's most important works and one of his first to break definitively with "neo-classic" tonality). A major turning point comes in the war-time settings from the Greek (translations by Ungaretti) for voice and instruments; quiet, intense, and persuasive, these small lyric works form simple, clear, twelve-tone structures. The two large post-war theatre works, the opera *Il Prigioniero* (completed in 1948) and the ballet *Job* (1950) are a deep plunge into the world of expressionism—undoubtedly facilitated by far greater contact with the music of the Viennese. Both these works are effective and powerful theatrical and human statements which gain strength, not from Dallapiccola's typical allusive lyricism (here much subordinated) but from a brilliant adaptation of twelve-tone ideas set forth in broad theatrical strokes. With the partial exception of the large-scale *Canti di liberazione* of 1955 (again a work with a "freedom" subject treated in terms of a simple, broad twelve-tone music for chorus and orchestra), the later works return to a lyric-elliptical style arising now, not from the theme of awakening consciousness in early antiquity (the Greek lyrics), but from the nature mysticism of medieval Italian religious poetry and the German romantic lyric.

A number of the younger and middle generation Italian composers with a basically diatonic and neo-classical style have introduced twelve-tone materials in their work. Goffredo Petrassi (b. 1904), whose earlier work was strictly neo-tonal in a Stravinskyian sense, has been using twelve-tone and serial material, first in a loose manner and without breaking the tonal bonds, later as a dominating factor. Petrassi's recent music abandons direct tonal techniques and approaches avant-garde serialism which in Italy, as elsewhere, had its point of departure in twelve-tone technique.

Both the musical style and the direct techniques of the Viennese school have had relatively limited overt influence in France. The conductor and composer René Leibowitz (b. 1913) was one of the first non-German composers to begin using twelve-tone ideas, and his book *Schoenberg et son école* (1947; in English, 1949) was one of the first in a non-German language; but Leibowitz's position in French music is today one of extreme isolation. Olivier Messiaen (b. 1908), who has put twelve-tone technique to his own purposes and abstracted serial ideas without relation to the style or esthetic of the Viennese, has proved to be a far more influential figure.

The transfer of Schoenberg's pupils Roberto Gerhard and Egon Wellesz (b. 1885) to England, the work of the Hungarian-British composer Mátyás Seiber (1905–1960), and the teaching and writing of the important theoretician, Hans Keller, had an influence on the development of English music somewhat analogous to that of European composers who came to the United States during the war. The first British composers to use twelve-tone technique were Elizabeth Lutyens (b. 1906), and Humphrey Searle (b. 1915), the latter a pupil of Webern although stylistically much closer to Berg. Other important twelve-tone composers in Great Britain include the Scottish composer Iain Hamilton (b. 1922), Alexander Goehr (b. 1932), and Peter Maxwell Davies (b. 1934) who, although at first associated with Central European avant-garde developments, has continued to follow a very personal small-scaled lyric twelve-tone style. Davies's output includes a number of pieces specifically intended for vocal and instrumental performance by children; they are among the rare examples of twelve-tone music not necessarily intended for professional performance. The Swedish composer, Karl-Birger Blomdahl (b. 1916), originally a neo-classicist, has developed a twelve-tone line of thought used rather strictly in a series of instrumental works, rather freely in a "space-ship" opera, *Aniara* (1959).

The influence and spread of twelve-tone ideas has been inhibited only in Eastern Europe where, until very recently at least officially controlled performance outlets have not accepted non-tonal, highly chromatic music for performance. The exception to this—and it is a major exception

—is Poland, where, since 1958, all forms of modern technique have received wide acceptance. After an initial impact of Bartók and Hindemith, the introduction of twelve-tone ideas materially changed the entire course of Polish contemporary music. Interestingly enough, a key work in this development was the *Funeral Music* (1958) of Witold Lutoslawski (b. 1913), dedicated to the memory of Béla Bartók and one of the first Polish works to make use of twelve-tone technique. Lutoslawski's music has developed through a chromatic, twelve-tone symphonic phase into a freer kind of avant-garde style laid out in broad rhythmic and color planes and blocked out in levels of intensity and timbre. Most of the younger Polish composers as well as Lutoslawski himself have moved well out of the area of closely controlled twelve-tone style and idea, but the block-like manipulation of large instrumental and orchestral intensities and timbres laid out in broad masses and dramatic juxtapositions has remained characteristic of recent Polish music. The direct techniques of twelve-tone music remain influential in the music of the older generation and in the work of a few of the important younger men: notably Tadeusz Baird (b. 1928), whose derivation from the Viennese is quite direct, and Kazimierz Serocki (b. 1922), who turned towards and then away from the rather static, dramatic-theatrical style of young Poland towards a new, on-going, developmental symphonic character often employing open or flexible materials but characterized by control.

Outside of Poland, the most important modern music center in Eastern Europe has been Yugoslavia, where a number of younger composers have been using contemporary ideas for several years; the best-known of these is Milko Kelemen (b. 1924), who has worked through the typical stylistic evolution from Bartók to Boulez with twelve-tone technique as a turning-point in between.

The situation all over Eastern Europe, however, is in flux and, with the exception of Albania, there is no country in that part of the world where the impact of rapid change is not being felt. Within a period that can almost be measured in months, avant-garde techniques—even extreme ones—have been taken up in nearly all of the major Eastern European centers. Twelve-tone technique has been adopted by composers even of the older generation in Czechoslovakia, Hungary, Rumania, and elsewhere. The Soviet Union has remained more isolated, but similar changes (at a more evolutionary pace, perhaps) are taking place there. Already over a period of years a number of Soviet composers have been working with twelve-tone and other contemporary materials, but this music has remained little known and little performed in or out of Russia. Among the best-known are the Muscovite Andrei Wolkonsky (b. 1916) and the Kiev composers Eddy Denisov and Valentin Silvestrov (b. 1937), whose twelve-tone chromatic styles suggest roots in Scriabin as well as Schoenberg and Berg. Among the younger generation are the Moscow composer Alfred Chnitke (b. 1934), who has been influenced by Boulez, and a

Lithuanian group including Arwo Pärt (b. 1935), who has created static color structures of considerable effectiveness.

The United States

The strongest line of continuity between the Viennese and latter-day twelve-tone composition is to be found in the United States, where Schoenberg settled in 1933 and remained as a teacher until his death in 1951. Schoenberg taught composers as disparate as Leon Kirchner and John Cage; and, indirectly, through the teaching and influence of a composer-teacher like Roger Sessions (b.1896), twelve-tone ideas became a dominant part of American music. In the 1920's, Sessions had developed a distinctive, rich, and contrapuntal neo-classical style later modified in the 1930's and 1940's into a characteristic, dense chromaticism of an expressive and individual character. This style, a personal way of speaking which, in works like the Violin Concerto (1935), the Symphony No. 2 (1945), and the opera The Trial of Lucullus (1947) can be easily differentiated from Viennese chromaticism, gradually absorbed constructive elements of row technique. Sessions's later works—particularly the Sonata for violin solo, (1953), the Piano Concerto (1956), the Idyll of Theocritus for voice and orchestra (1956), the Symphony No. 4 (1958), and the opera Montezuma (1947–1962)—are dominated by row material which adds constructive strength and solidity while actually reinforcing the sense of stylistic identity and individuality. The primary impulse of Sessions's music—and in this he resembles Schoenberg—is contrapuntal; it is the characteristic web of long, shaped lines which gives the typical sound to the music. But Sessions's line is also concrete in conception, vocal in shape, and dependent on a complex sense of phrase accent and motion which gives a dynamic impulse to the music remarkably parallel to the way that classical harmonic progressions performed the same function.

This characteristic linear chromaticism dominates the work of a large group of American composers, many of whom studied with Sessions—Andrew Imbrie (b. 1921), Seymour Shifrin (b. 1926), Leon Kirchner (b. 1919) are outstanding examples. Composers like Ben Weber (b. 1916) and George Rochberg (b. 1918) have been working on essentially independent, parallel lines.[1] All of these are basically twelve-tone composers, with the exception of Kirchner, whose music derives directly from the chromatic expressionism of the Viennese and the pre-twelve-tone Sessions. Chromatic idioms (mainly but not exclusively twelve-tone) based on a "narrative," on-going phrase structure and some kind of contrapuntal, developmental form are the norm in American music today just as "neo-

---

[1] Rochberg's more recent work, however, uses quotation-collage techniques.

classicism" or some kind of "neo-tonality" was ten and twenty years ago.

These large-scale directional-developmental or narrative forms which replace the old functional tonality by some kind of row thinking stand in contrast to a number of important recent works which interpret twelve-tone ideas in terms of static, suspended structures which interlock in various cyclical patterns; these have, in fact, a relationship with certain "neo-classic" structural (as opposed to stylistic) notions, now newly propounded in terms of the chromatic material. The late music of Stravinsky himself belongs here, along with a number of parallel (and, in some cases, earlier) twelve-tone pieces by American composers whose work has been identified with his, notably Aaron Copland and Arthur Berger. Copland's involvement with chromatic techniques goes back to the 1920's; his *Piano Variations* of 1930 employ very closely worked and effective serial techniques based on a four-note row that is, in type, not at all unlike certain ideas used by Webern. Copland returned to this kind of serial, chromatic material in 1950 with his Piano Quartet and again with the *Piano Fantasy* of 1960 and the *Connotations for Orchestra* of 1962. They are strongly twelve-tone in sound and method although expressing characteristic Copland techniques of layers and planes, angles, and juxtapositions; these conceptual principles even carry over into a recent non-twelve-tone work like the *Nonet for Strings* of 1960. Arthur Berger, whose earlier music was strongly "neo-classic," developed a technique for projecting long-range linear motion—chromatic and contrapuntal—in terms of big blocked-out static structures which themselves interlock through internal twelve-tone relationships. In his first works of this kind (e.g., the *Chamber Music for 13 Instruments* of 1956) these techniques are specifically adapted to neo-classic rhythmic and phrase structures. Later (in the String Quartet of 1959, for example), this "neo-classicism" disappears or is absorbed into larger patterns; the detail is chromatic, highly inventive and serial-twelve-tone; the big forms remain sectional and additive in the neo-classic sense but are made organic by being interpenetrated by the row and the row-sound.

Stravinsky's original involvement with row technique was with the serial-order principle—the tenor solo in the *Cantata* (1951–1952), the Septet (1952–1953), the Shakespeare songs (1954) and *In Memoriam Dylan Thomas* (1954) are based on rows, but they are not twelve-tone. Only later and through his specific interest in a technical-structural idea —not altogether unrelated to quasi-serial techniques he had earlier developed for detail patterns and even (as in the *Symphony of Psalms*) for longer-range relationships—did Stravinsky begin to work with the full chromatic material. The score for the ballet *Agon* (1957) actually sums up the process as part of its own developing form: it begins diatonically, becomes chromatic and twelve-tone, and eventually returns to the diatonicism of the opening. A similar and even more wide-ranging process takes place in *Canticum Sacrum* (1956), a work which moves from Gregorian intonation to dodecaphony. Since 1958, however, Stravinsky's music has been strictly twelve-tone although, to be sure, always in a very distinctly Stravinskyian way. *Threni* (1958), a large-scale work for soloists, chorus, and orchestra, is completely organized in twelve-tone fashion not only in matters of detail but in the way the larger plan relates to that detail; for example, points of major articulation are often as clearly organized with respect to one another as are the smaller events in between. The result—particularly in the choral and vocal writing—has the effect of a series of unyielding statements (big choral declarations, *a cappella* solo voices in canon, etc.) with a sparse ornamental detail which, in effect, represent a transformation into twelve-tone thinking of Stravinsky's characteristic underlying formal and esthetic sense. Stravinsky's dodecaphonic music is neo-twelve-tone in the same sense that his earlier works are neo-tonal—"neo-classic" or "neo-baroque." *Movements* for piano and orchestra (1958–1959) stands in the same relationship to the music of Anton Webern as the *Dumbarton Oaks Concerto* and *The Rake's Progress* do to the works of Bach and Mozart. Neither in the latter nor the former case is there any question of a model but rather of the materials of a discourse whose actual forms—propositions and conclusions—are, as always, quite personal and original.

After *Movements* Stravinsky again turned to vocal and vocal-dramatic materials in a series of spare, aphoristic works—*A Sermon, A Narrative, and a Prayer; The Dove Descending Breaks the Air* for *a cappella* chorus; a short work in memory of President Kennedy; the television dance-drama *The Flood; Abraham and Isaac*, a Biblical setting in Hebrew for baritone and orchestra. Virtually all of these unite a special permutational twelve-tone technique, a pointed thinness and brevity, a kind of abstracted religious mysticism expressed in a contemporary twelve-tone stylization and sometimes—especially in a long vocal incantation like *Abraham and Isaac* —worked into long lines of great beauty. There is no reason to think that these compositions mark the final evolution of Stravinsky's work; quite the contrary, there is evidence—in the orchestral Variations—of a new development towards sonority and richness. But Stravinsky's unexpected turn towards the twelve-tone idea, treated in his own personal manner, was a remarkable demonstration of the essential unity underlying apparently dissimilar and contradictory twentieth-century art.

Bibliography:

An extensive bibliography of writings on twelve-tone, serial, and electronic music by Ann Basart was published by the U. of California Press in 1962. Roman Vlad's *Storia della dodecafonia* (Milan, 1958) is one of the few general sources which discuss the diffusion of twelve-tone ideas; however, it contains nothing about American music and is not translated. The best source of specific information about American twelve-tone music is to be found in various articles in *Perspectives of New Music*. Milton Babbitt's "Remarks on the Recent Stravinsky" in the Spring–Summer, 1964, issue of that magazine, concerns the serial Stravinsky; Peter Evans's discussion of the Copland twelve-tone *Connotations* appears in the same issue.

12

Before World War II;
The Sources

The development of new musical ideas since World War II has, in spite of great diversity, taken on certain characteristic forms: the isolation of the individual acoustical event; the extension of the sound material to include the entire possible range of aural sensation; the absolutely equal esthetic (though not necessarily equal artistic, psychological or psycho-acoustical) validity of all possible material in all possible aspects (duration or loudness, for example, being of a significance at least equal to fixed pitch). Every level of performance control is possible, from total deter-minism to improvisation or to random choice within open patterns whose shape and content may be determined at any level, at any time before or during the performance, and to any extent; all relationships (including none) are possible.

In one sense, the avant-gardism of recent years is a continuation of motifs begun early in the twentieth century and interrupted by the achievement of closed, settled forms in the middle and late works of composers like Stravinsky and Schoenberg. The freely atonal works of the Viennese and music like that of *Le Sacre* tend, not only towards the development of new, non-tonal materials, but also towards organic, non-developmental forms either on the static, "additive" Stravinskyian model or on that of the associative on-going form often credited to Debussy but also significantly developed by Schoenberg in a work like *Erwartung*. The line of thought proposed by Schoenberg in early and late works and by Webern was especially significant, not only for brevity and concision of form, but also for the way individual events were broken down and isolated into clear, differentiated packets of sound with clearly identifiable characteristics which suggested the possibility of restocking and rebuilding the entire process of creative thought from its basic elements. The specific order or serial principles of twelve-tone music, especially as extended to encompass not only pitch but also duration, dynamics, and even timbre, were decisive in the development of a great deal of post-war musical thinking.

There were, however, other antecedents. The Futurists (who gave concerts of noises before World War I and who had an influence on Varèse) and the Dadaists (Marcel Duchamp's *Erratum musical* of 1913 consists of random isolated pitches without any indicated durations) gave performances which included musical and sound manifestations of various kinds; the concepts of chance and open form have relatively long and honorable literary histories (see for example the ideas of Mallarmé, which had a great influence on Boulez). Next to the expansion and development of chromatic, rhythmic, and timbral ideas in Vienna and Paris, however, the most important experimental and path-breaking musical work was in the United States. American musical culture in the nineteenth century was, on the surface at least, largely imported from Europe, although 3,000 miles of ocean, a rather lively folk tradition (also imported but with pre-tonal features and developed here in a distinctive way), and the conservation and new growth of improvisational styles and techniques kept a non-European line alive. The special use of non-tempered pitches in the "blues" tradition, of rhythmic flexibility and asymmetrical phrase structure (although set on top of a steady harmonic and metrical beat), of on-going structure, of extreme virtuosity and unconventional instrumental resources—all these aspects of the jazz experience also had significance for the distinctive development of an American music.

Ives

The first composer whose work stands essentially outside the received

European tradition was Charles Ives (1874–1954). Ives was a great original working far from the European centers and years ahead of the European innovators. He composed proto-serial and proto-aleatory music; he invented block forms and free forms; he used tone clusters and structural densities; he wrote in poly-meters and poly-tempi; he composed spatial music and music that could be realized in a multiplicity of ways; he anticipated recent improvisatory works-in-progress, assemblages, and "pop-art" ideas—in short, just about every important development of the last sixty years and some of the most notable of the last fifteen. Yet Ives was also, in a way, a traditionalist, and he used aspects of American and European tradition throughout his creative work. In one sense, he stood so far outside of these traditions (although he understood them perfectly well) that —unlike Schoenberg and Stravinsky—he did not have to overthrow them and then labor mightily to rebuild. He knew and used what he needed in just the same casual, determined way he used any idea or material that was appropriate or relevant to what he had to say. Ives felt no "historical compulsion" to abandon tonality (or anything else); his music turns away from narrative and process in the conventional sense; its tendency is inclusive; it absorbs or even revels in contradictions. Like Whitman, Ives could contradict himself, he could contain multitudes.

Nothing in human experience was alien to Ives, but that does not mean that he was a "primitive." There is a myth which depicts him as an untutored pioneer in the New England wilderness; a visionary but a kind of musical Grandma Moses; a rugged individualist working in complete isolation, utterly lacking in technical skill and sophistication but totally original in a rough and ready way; a kind of inspired *naïf*; a phenomenon of nature. In actual fact, Ives's father was a well-known bandmaster who did many experiments in acoustics and temperament. Ives studied with his father in his hometown of Danbury and later at Yale with the distinguished Horatio Parker. He had extensive practical experience with his father's band, arranging for it and playing with theatre orchestras and on church organs in New Haven and New York. All of Ives's mature life and most of his composing years were spent, not in the wilderness, but in New York where he embarked on a double career as an extremely successful insurance broker and a composer. Most of his music was actually written between his arrival in New York in 1898 and a period shortly after World War I; he spent the later years of life arranging, putting in order and preparing for performance works taken from the enormous mass of material which he had produced earlier.

None of this is meant to detract from Ives's stature as an innovator or as an individualist; quite the contrary, it should emphasize his real achievement by taking it out of the realm of nature mythology and emphasizing its origins in conscious decision and choice. For example, Ives was always able to use tradition—classical tonality, say—in exactly the same way he used his own new tonalities, poly-tonalities and non-tonalities, is a kind of special case, as it were, of our total experience of meaningful sound. It was this range of activity, this totality of experience that interested Ives and it was out of this totality of experience—out of simplicity and complexity, coherence and contradiction—that he made his pieces. One of his best-known pieces, *The Unanswered Question*, shows his technique of deriving a completely new form out of simple, contradictory elements. A small group of strings—it can be merely a string quartet—is seated off-stage or away from the other instruments; it provides an obsessive, endless rotation of a simple "chorale" sequence of triadic harmonies. On another level, entirely detached from the strings and without any specific rhythmic coordination, a trumpet plays a constantly reiterated rising inflection. Opposite, flutes (possibly mixed with an oboe and a clarinet) respond to the trumpet question, toss it around, and eventually get into a terrible tangle (Example 12-1). There is, in the end, no answer, no resolution; only the question unchanged and the distant string "harmony of the spheres" fading out to infinity.

This tiny conception is full of prophetic Ivesianisms: the literary idea which generates a form; the unification of seemingly contradictory material through the very exploitation of the fact of contradiction; the easily perceptible external references; the spatial arrangement of the instruments; the projection of distinct layers of sound with informal vertical arrangements. What is not so obvious is just how all these elements come together to make an expressive form which communicates on a subtler level by no means equivalent to the verbal descriptions.

The Ivesian view of art and life has to do with the value of a poetic idea realized as a human action or activity. In spite of all his presumed impracticality (many of the old difficulties of performance, of notation, and of general comprehensibility have, of course, vanished over the years), Ives thought of his music as a kind of non-passive, performance-practice activity; he meant it primarily to be performed, only secondarily to be listened to and even then in an active, participating way. He seems to have had the idea that audiences might, at some point, sing along or that someone might jump up with a flute or a mouth harmonica and join in. Ives wanted to transform even the passive state of reception into positive involvement, which accounts in part for the intentional use of familiar and popular music to produce the shock of surprise or amused recognition. Yet, on the other hand, he hardly even "composed" music in the usual sense. During his creative years, he poured out a continuous stream of musical expression—works for chorus and organ, five symphonies, four sonatas for violin and piano, two string quartets, many piano works including the massive "Concord" Sonata, a large number of songs, and extremely important works for chamber orchestra or chamber ensemble: the sets of *Tone Roads, Three Places in New England, Central Park in the Dark, Over the Pavements*. There is no question that Ives knew what he wanted in these works—he claimed to have tried many of

EXAMPLE 12.1. Ives, *The Unanswered Question*. Used by permission. Copyright 1953 by Southern Music Publishing Co., Inc.

his ideas out in practice during his theatre orchestra and organist days and, by accounts, he could show what he wanted on the piano. On the other hand, what he wanted was often intentionally unclear or imprecise, and he himself changed the way he played his music over the years. His idea was to involve the performer in the activity of creating the music, and the works themselves form a kind of continuous stream of musical expression, portions of which have coalesced—indeed are still coalescing—into individual scores.

Ives disliked and distrusted the conventionalized rituals of public music-making; he wanted to get back to some underlying realities about human activity, about the physical reality of human beings communicating immediate and almost tangible experiences—even experiences of complexity, contradiction, and incoherence. He wanted a speaking kind of music, a music that could be jotted down to convey fresh impressions and thoughts, that could flow with the naturalness of plain speech; a music that could somehow get across that impenetrable barrier between art and life, not to "express" nature but to flow along as part of it. On the one hand, he wrote music that was and is difficult, every part a separate and individual activity; on the other, he wrote things that are easy and banal. He was wildly visionary; one music runs exaltedly or humorously into the next, and only with the greatest difficulty could performable pieces be separated out and extracted in a practical, usable state. Yet there is nothing abstract about any of Ives; all of it is conceived, not as paper music, but as matter for action. He wanted performers to decipher illegible and complex new notations, but he also wanted them to understand his ideas and ideals and act freely within them. He wanted to speak to those who understood, yet he also thought that anyone could understand and he wanted everyone to participate. He was not himself a "phenomenon of nature," but he wanted to think of his music that way. He wanted to break down the distinctions between man and nature, between art and life, to integrate them into some all-embracing experience. His last piece was to be a "Universe" Symphony to be played and sung in the fields and mountains by thousands—indeed, by all of humanity.

Ives's music has had a direct and continuing influence and can be linked quite directly with certain recent avant-garde ideas. On the other hand, he was also a kind of traditionalist—if one realizes that Ives and his father were the only important musical representatives of that tradition! The tradition was, of course, that of Whitman, of Thoreau, Emerson and the New England "transcendentalists," and Ives set himself the job of creating, single-handed, a musical equivalent. This tradition, above all others, had to find its starting points in some kind of expression that was at once personal, free, and spontaneous, close to "natural" expression. Ives's range runs from hymn tunes and ragtimes to complex, atonal polyphonies; he had to compose out the entire tradition from one end to the other. At the same time, he was able to encompass his vision of the totality of human experience within a personal utterance which was also an evocation of some Golden Age in which art and life were—or would be—naturally and inextricably woven together.

Other innovators; Varèse

The period of the 1920's was one of extensive exploration in American music, and the intensity and importance of the activity has scarcely any parallel in the European music of the time (a similar kind of activity seems to have existed in the young Soviet Union, but years of Stalinism all but obliterated even the very names of pioneers such as Rosslavetz). The creation and assimilation of new ideas was a primary aim, and the strong musical voices were recognizably those dealing most directly with new materials and new ways of organizing sound: Edgard Varèse (1883–1965). Henry Cowell (1897–1965), Carl Ruggles (b. 1876), George Antheil (1900–1959), and, of course, Ives. The works of Wallingford Riegger (1885–1961) and Adolph Weiss (b. 1891), Leo Ornstein (b. 1895; a Russian-born American who specialized in thick cluster dissonance and static accentual forms), John J. Becker (1886–1961) and Ruth Crawford Seeger (1901–1953; her husband, Charles Seeger, was an important theorist of new resources and Mrs. Seeger's remarkable String Quartet of 1931 is, as an example, full of proto-serialism) extend and diffuse the experimental tradition well into the 1930's and 1940's. Copland's music of the 1920's and early 1930's was strongly influenced by the current avant-garde ideas; it is curious to realize that the position of Roger Sessions was, with respect to the American modernist movements of the day, quite conservative. Ideas such as tone clusters, new scalar and rhythmic formations, new notations, new instruments, and especially, new mechanical techniques were very much in the air. In an entire issue devoted to the new mechanical and electronic techniques, the composers' journal *Modern Music* clearly anticipated the whole idea of *musique concrète* ("Recorded Noises—Tomorrow's Instrumentation") as well as certain aspects of electronic music ("electrical musical instruments" or "eminos").

Some of these pioneers have remained essentially isolated figures without—until now—significant influence. Antheil, who made something of a European reputation with a wild-man, banging-on-the-piano style, attracted a great deal of attention with his *Ballet mécanique* (1925), a work scored for percussion, player pianos, the sound of airplane motors, and so forth; the piece, although still attractive, seems tame enough today and its importance has been eclipsed by more remarkable percussion works such as Varèse's *Ionisation*. Antheil's later music—much of it written for Hollywood—was tonal, conservative, and mild. On the other hand, Ruggles has remained the classic type of American rugged individualist; at 90, he still lives in his New England retreat, still paints and composes his rare dense, personal, chromatic music—*Angels* (1920), *Men and Mountains* (1924), *Portals* (1926), *Sun-Treader* (1933), *Evocations* (1937–1945), and *Organum* (1945). To some extent, this tradition of isolated, eccentric individualism has survived in the personalities of composers like Henry Brant (b. 1913) and Harry Partch (b. 1901). Brant, a former jazz arranger now teaching at Bennington College, anticipated current avant-garde ideas in creating open rhythmic structures ("poly-chronic," that is, in independent, multiple meters and tempos) set into giant, freely coordinated spatial counterpoints which derive ultimately from Ives. Brant creates out of the character of instruments, their physical disposition, and the acoustical properties of the space in which they are enclosed; typically, he distributes instruments around a hall with groups working individually on flexible material in a free, even unco-ordinated stereophony. He has also proposed a kind of collective performance-practice ideal and has proposed a method of teaching music through creative activity. Partch has developed a microtonal music using a series of special and remarkable instruments created for his purposes. The conception of microtonal music is far from new (non-tempered divisions of the octave exist in most non-Western musical cultures) but, along with the Czech Alois Hába (who has now apparently largely abandoned it), the Mexican Julian Carrillo and the Russian Vyshnegradsky, Partch is one of the few composers who have pursued the subject systematically and creatively; microtonal materials and techniques, although common in electronic music, have had only peripheral use in instrumental writing and remain essentially undeveloped resources.[1]

The most important composer on the American avant-garde scene in the 1920's was certainly Edgard Varèse—and, after a period of eclipse, he again became part of the mainstream of new ideas. Varèse was born and educated in France but he came to New York in 1915 and all his mature work was associated with his adopted country. Varèse was perhaps the first composer to conceive of sound conglomerations as objects essentially remote from the traditional possibility of development and variation. In a series of works beginning with *Offrandes* of 1921 and continuing with *Hyperprism* (1922), *Octandre* (1924), and *Intégrales* (1924), all for chamber orchestra, *Amériques* (1922) and *Arcana* (1927) for large orchestra, Varèse created a type of static, spatial music which gradually detaches itself almost completely from thematic construction of any kind. The materials become almost totally non-linear. The "melodic" fixed-pitch content often reduces itself to insistent groupings of repeated notes; two- and three-note groups are repeated over and over in differing rhythmic guises while clusters of vertical dissonances stab through a percussive texture. The harmonic content has little to do with "chords" and progressions in the usual sense; these agglomerations of instrumental sonorities and

---

[1] Microtonal techniques are still being used, notably by Ben Johnston, at the University of Illinois where Partch was formerly in residence.

densities function as texture and color. Indeed, the real subject matter of this music is texture, color, accent, and dynamic, all heard as aspects of a basic unity. Percussive rhythm becomes melody, melody becomes accent and sonority. The materials consist of fixed, invented musical shapes, powerful, static blocks of sound piled up in great, spatial juxtapositions and defining a new, imagined musical space. The structures are almost literally held together by a kind of inner tension; enormous amounts of static energy are present, but the more energy expended, the more seems to be created. There is no sense of motion in the conventional sense at all but rather a play of potential and kinetic energies which give the impression of holding together complex, unyielding physical sound objects set, as it were, into a dynamic musical space.

These concepts are, in fact, among the intellectual and musical foundations for the post-war percussion music and for many of the basic ideas of tape and electronic music as well. Varèse's tendency had long been to treat pitch as an aspect of timbre and accent in a kind of continuum between fixed pitch on the one hand and rhythm and accent on the other. But, if pitch is no longer the on-going, developmental, all-powerful generator of form, it is by no means abandoned, even in an all-percussion piece like the famous *Ionisation* of 1931. On the contrary, the use of the siren—i.e. of pitch varying at a constant rate on a continuum—and the structurally important, climactic entrance of the piano and bells near the end of *Ionisation* (Example 12-2) are striking examples of how pitch is used in a new way, as a structurally defining element in a piece primarily based on color and accent (it is, in a way, the exact reverse of the way rhythm and accent are often structurally defining elements in music based on fixed pitch values). It was perfectly possible for Varèse, only a few years later, to write a wholly successful work for solo flute—his famous *Density 21.5* —with a completely original, expressive, and integrated conception of a single, pitched instrumental line.

An important relationship exists between the ideas of Varèse and the *musique concrète* of the post-war period. *Musique concrète*, which was developed by a group of technicians at the French National Radio in 1948, is fundamentally a sound-montage idea based on the use of recorded noises. The work of Pierre Schaeffer and his colleagues has not proved to be musically significant, but in one general respect its importance was overwhelming; *musique concrète* established definitively the fact that all possible aural sensations were now available for creative use as raw material. This possibility was foreseen many years ago by Varèse, not merely as an endless reservoir of new resources, but as the basis for the construction of new forms relevant to and expressive of contemporary experience; fittingly, it was Varèse who provided the *musique concrète* movement with its only masterpieces to date: *Déserts* (1954), for tape and instrumental ensemble, and *Poème électronique*, commissioned for the 400-odd loudspeakers that sent sound spinning around the inside of Le Corbusier's Philips Pavilion at

EXAMPLE 12-2. Varèse, *Ionisation*, excerpt. © 1934 by Edgard Varèse. By permission of Franco Colombo, Inc., Publisher.

the 1958 Brussels World's Fair. These powerful collages are worked ou
of pre-existing recorded sound material built up into new spatial structure
of great originality, breadth, and scope. A work like the *Poème*, althougl
designed for a continuous stereophony, is overwhelming even heard in
mere two channels; the spatial concept is not merely a matter of th
physical arrangement of the sound sources; it is actually built into th
juxtapositions of aural images, slowly turning and colliding in cataclysmi
spatial encounters.

Henry Cowell was the most direct representative of the Ives traditior
in the 1920's, the most important link between Ives and the latter-day
avant-garde, and one of the most prolific innovators of the century
Cowell's work is a vast accumulation of new materials and ideas; the mos
famous of these, the "tone cluster," is simply an agglomeration of adjacen
fixed frequencies in which, however, the over-all impression is that of ;
texture rather than of a chordal sonority consisting of separable pitcl
elements. The "cluster" occupies an intermediate ground between fixec
pitch and noise: it is made up of fixed frequencies, but the complex anc

EXAMPLE 12-3. Cowell, "Tiger." Quoted by permission of Associated Music Publishers, Inc.

confused interaction of the upper partials of these frequencies produces an indeterminate effect closely related to noise. Cowell's *Mosaic* for string quartet and *26 Simultaneous Mosaics* for five players are remarkable early examples of open form. He also did extensive and important creative investigation in the field of rhythm and was perhaps the first person to propose —and realize in a piece of music—the concept of deriving rhythmic-durational relationships from the ratios of harmonic vibrations (2:1, 3:2, 4:3, etc.). Cowell also developed a great number of new instrumental resources—most notably, a great variety of timbres plucked, scraped, strummed, and scratched out of the insides of the piano—and he pioneered in new notational techniques appropriate to his new resources (Example 12-3). His later work tended to be more concerned with materials drawn from folk, "ethnic," and non-Western sources treated in terms of Western instrumental and musical organizations.

Cowell's work provides an immediate connection between the experimental activities of the 1920's and the rather special, quiet, and mild avant-garde movements of the American 1930's and 1940's. These developments, which were centered in Cowell's home state of California, had two closely related aspects. One was the conscious development of non-Western materials, ranging in origin from Bali to Armenia; the other, related to certain developments in Cuba and Mexico, was the extensive use of percussion instruments and percussion ensembles (Cowell, Lou Harrison, Colin Mc-Phee, Alan Hovhaness, John Cage). The best-known figure to emerge from this group is John Cage (b. 1912). Cage's initial preoccupations were with Oriental ideas and with percussion music; *Double Music* for percussion ensemble was written in collaboration with Lou Harrison, and the famous "prepared piano" was a way of achieving a wide range of percussion effects with a single performer and a single instrument. An important aspect of the California Oriental-percussion music and of Cage's contributions was the denial of the traditional supremacy of pitch organization in Western music. Cage later went on to deny the relationship between one sound event and another, and ultimately even the conscious determination and control of such events.

Bibliography

Duchamp's *Erratum musical* is given in Robert Lebel's *Marcel Duchamp*, transl. G. H. Hamilton (New York, 1959).

For Ives, see his own *Essays Before a Sonata*, reprinted in the *Three Classics* previously cited and in a volume edited by Howard Boatwright (New York, 1961); also Henry and Sidney Cowell, *Charles Ives and His Music* (New York, 1955).

Cowell's *New Musical Resources* (New York, 1930) and the essays he edited under the title *American Composers on American Music* (1933; reprinted New York, 1962) are basic documents for the American 1920's and 1930's, as are the issues of *Modern Music* and the *Copland on Music* volume already cited. George Antheil's *Bad Boy of Music* (New York, 1945) is an anecdotal autobiography.

Tragically little material on Varèse has been published, although the French-Canadian review, *Libertés,* devoted an issue to him and his pupil Chou Wen–chung is compiling an extensive Varèse documentation.

13
Ultra-Rationality and Electronic Music

The creation of *musique concrète* in Paris, Cage's first experiments with chance, randomness, and indeterminacy, and the concept of a totally organized, totally rational music were almost simultaneous events. Suddenly, after the war, the expansion of materials, techniques, and new perceptive forms, initiated in the earlier years of the century and long interrupted, resumed with an unparalleled force and pace. The developments of the late 1940's and early 1950's, curiously parallel and mutually exclusive, grew out of the necessity to discover and nourish new bits of experience and new ways of experiencing, all rigorously pushed to their logical and physical extremes, much in the manner of scientific experimentation.

Babbitt and serialism

Even from its first appearance, the twelve-tone idea was never merely a matter of pitch arrangement; the order principle inevitably affected and was intertwined with the rhythmic, dynamic, and even timbral character of the music. More specifically, Webern and—as is often overlooked—Schoenberg established a carefully coordinated set of relationships, not only between the parts, but between the various aspects or dimensions of the musical discourse. However, the first compositions in which linear succession, harmonic simultaneity, duration (including rhythm and tempo), dynamics, articulation, register, and timbre are all strictly derived from a single, all-inclusive premise, were written in 1948 by Milton Babbitt (b. 1916): his *Three Compositions* for piano[1] and his *Compositions* for four instruments and for twelve instruments. With Schoenberg and even Webern, the twelve-tone idea remains essentially a process or, to use Schoenberg's own term, a method. With Babbitt, it is most definitely and carefully a "system" in the strictest sense. The row becomes a "set" of values and relationships, absolutely and strictly defined not only in terms of structure but also of operational process. Thus, the twelve-tone material represents the totality of possible relationships inherent in every aspect of the musical material, and the actual unfolding of each piece is a process of permutation within which all these potential relationships are revealed.

In the late 1950's, Babbitt began working at the newly reorganized Columbia-Princeton Electronic Music Center with the R.C.A. Electronic Sound Synthesizer. Electronic music—as distinguished from recorded-sound, collage techniques such as *musique concrète*—is based on the simple principle that the electromagnetic impulses which are used to drive a loud-speaker in the *reproduction* of live sound can also be utilized to produce sound—"artificially," and by totally electronic means. The development of electronic techniques in Europe and the United States is discussed at some length below; here let it suffice to say that the R.C.A. Synthesizer is a sophisticated instrument specifically constructed for the production of synthesized electronic sound. Every aspect of both pitched and non-pitched sound—including duration, quality of attack and decay (dying away), intensity, tone color, and so forth—can be set out with precise definition, and any sound can be tested immediately and, if necessary, re-adjusted down to the finest possible gradations. Babbitt's interest in electronic techniques has not been so much in matters of new sounds but rather in the possibilities of control, and his electronic works—*Composition for Synthesizer, Ensembles for Synthesizer*—have been primarily concerned with new ways of organizing time and form perception.

As with others of his contemporaries, Babbitt's electronic experience seems to have affected the character of his "live" performed music, which

---

[1] Although, in this work, the premise is not quite yet all-inclusive.

as taken on a new vitality and color. Works like *All Set* for jazz ensemble, *Partitions* for piano, and *Sounds and Words* for soprano and piano combine Babbitt's typical clarity and care with a new richness and lively virtuosity appropriate to the conditions of live performance. Babbitt has also now twice combined live performance with tape in a pair of works for soprano and synthesizer: a setting of Dylan Thomas' *Vision and Prayer* with a purely "synthesized" accompaniment, and *Philomel*, a setting of a text by John Hollander using live voice, recorded vocal material, and purely electronic sound (Example 13-1). The Greek legend of Philomel, the maiden who was ravished, and her tongue torn out, and then, through the pity of the Gods, was turned into a nightingale, suggests a unity of poetic and musical expression; in the Babbitt-Hollander piece, language becomes a kind of musical expression while the music becomes articulate and precise, almost like language. Inarticulateness and the quality of musical experience itself are made rational and, as in all of Babbitt's work but perhaps with the greatest force in *Philomel*, the range of perceptive experi-

EXAMPLE 13-1. Babbitt, *Philomel*, excerpt. Quoted by permission of Associated Music Publishers, Inc.

EXAMPLE 13-1 continued.

ence and the utter clarity and control of this experience quite literally "express" complex, non-verbal thought processes.

Babbitt has had a strong influence as a teacher and theoretician, primarily in the United States. The most skillful of Babbitt's pupils—Donald Martino, Henry Weinberg, Peter Westergaard—have developed individual means and styles of considerable originality within the premises of total rationality. Babbitt's influence seems most significant, not so much in specific matters of method and style, as in the more general diffusion of concepts of technique and of intellectual responsibility.

European serialism

The first "totally organized" piece of music to be written in Europe was the étude, *Mode de valeurs et d'intensité*, one of a set of piano pieces written by Olivier Messiaen in 1949. Messiaen (b. 1908) has a particular place in recent musical history as a genial and eccentric figure who has produced a remarkable, highly original, flawed body of work. Primary sources of Messiaenic inspiration are bird calls—he is an expert musical ornithologist and his bird songs are authentic—and rhythmic modes of presumably "Oriental" derivation; to this can be added twelve-tone technique; a concept of sonority and static, spatial form akin to Varèse's; and more than a touch of religious, medieval mysticism, plainsong included. There is an exceptional quality of concreteness (one would almost say tangibility) in the sonorous fantasies of works like the *Oiseaux exotiques* of 1956 and (to a lesser degree) the *Chronochromie* for orchestra of 1960. Messiaen's importance as a teacher and as an influence on the younger European composers has been enormous; after the war, he was one of the few European musicians who taught twelve-tone technique, the first to relate pitch serialization with organized rhythm, and almost the only one who was entirely free, not only of the prejudices of the tonal system, but of the orthodoxies of the Schoenberg followers as well. Messiaen was the teacher of Pierre Boulez and Karlheinz Stockhausen and thus became the father of recent European avant-garde music.

The most powerful impulse in the initial development of new ideas in post-World War II Europe was the re-appearance of twelve-tone technique. Whereas the development of twelve-tone ideas was fairly continuous in the United States, it was completely cut off in Europe by the crises of the 1930's and the war. The first task of the younger European composers—and, for that matter, many of the older ones—was the rediscovery of the one technique that seemed to offer a means of expressing new ideas in new ways; hence the great importance of a handful of teachers like Messiaen and of the newly created international school and festival at Darmstadt where the long-suppressed music of Schoenberg and Webern could be heard and their techniques studied. It was Webern's work rather than Schoenberg's which showed the way: Webern seemed to offer the possibility of building a new music from the simplest and barest of premises; the younger European composers—Boulez, Stockhausen, the Italians Luigi Nono, Bruno Maderna, and Luciano Berio—began as Webernists. Their initial premises were the individual isolated sound event and the rational, organizing power of the serial principle; they did not hesitate to draw the most extreme conclusions from these simple propositions. The twelve-tone idea in pieces like Boulez's *Structures* for two pianos or Stockhausen's *Kontrapunkte* is not (in Schoenberg's sense) a method nor (in Babbitt's sense) a complex system but rather a total generating principle through which a new and complete identity of materials, means, structure, and expression could, hopefully, be achieved. The difficulty with this identity was always that it remained, even in the best examples, a mere play of numbers arbitrarily translated into various musical facts, without a real organic base in perceptive experience. But it also gave rise to the characteristic European "serialism" with its idea of a fixed scale of values.

In serialism's simple early form, the twelve-tone arrangement of the pitches was paralleled by an arrangement of twelve durations, a fixed grouping of twelve dynamic values, and so forth. All of the possible points of intersection of these values could then be plotted; the result was the piece.[2] The reign of this strict and narrow interpretation of serial technique was in fact rather brief, although literally dozens and even hundreds of totally organized, post-Webern serial pieces were written, nearly all for small combinations of instruments and nearly all based on a highly rationalized arrangement of isolated, "pointillist" events and textures, often surrounded by generous amounts of highly organized silence.

The initial impulses towards this refined, ultra-rational post-Webernism came from Messiaen and Boulez in Paris; a second group of composers in Northern Italy—most importantly Luigi Nono—came out of the Webern-Dallapiccola line under the direct influence and tutelage of the German conductor Herman Scherchen, one of the few musical personalities who represent a line between the Viennese School and the post-war avant-garde. But the most important architect and theorist of European serial ideas was, and remains, Karlheinz Stockhausen. Stockhausen's initial concerns were the complete isolation and definition of every aspect of musical sound and the extension of serial control into every domain. The latter point is important; Stockhausen envisaged the possibility of serializing and thus pre-controlling even such matters as the density of harmonic, vertical masses; the number of musical events occurring in given time segments; the size of intervals and the choice of register; the types of attacks and articulations employed; the rate of change of texture and tone color. Often the technique and the formal ideas far outrun the actual materials; in the *Klavierstücke I-IV* (1952–1953), for example, there are combinations or refined distinctions which cannot be meaningfully realized. Later, Stockhausen was to return to performed music with new ways of applying serial technique to the necessities of live performance; in the early 1950's, however, electronic music seemed to offer the solution to the serial dilemma.

Electronic music

The Cologne Electronic Studio was initiated in 1951 under the direction of Herbert Eimert (b. 1897) with the aim of exploring the electronic generation of sound. Purely electronic production of sound was not a new idea, for the Hammond organ, the Theremin, the Ondes Martenot, and similar inventions were all electronic adaptations of the conventional idea of a musical instrument. Now, however, the vast improvement in amplification and speaker systems and the widespread availability of a faithful, durable, and easily handled storage device—magnetic tape—made it possible for the composer to establish the fixed and final form of his

[2] It is not quite accurate to say, as some commentators have, that this is music in which analysis *precedes* composition. The analysis is quite equivalent to the piece.

creation by working directly on the medium and without the aid of an interpreter. In a strict sense, pure electronic music is based on the premise that a loud-speaker can be driven to produce sound by electromagnetic impulses derived (with or without the intermediary technique of tape storage) from electronic generators; these generators produce impulses ranging from the simple pulse of a sine wave (producing a "pure" sinusoidal tone) to the complex, random oscillation of all the audible frequencies (producing the great grand-daddy of all sound, "white noise"). By contrast (although the distinction has been somewhat outmoded by an almost universal tendency to mix materials), the use of recorded "real" sounds falls into the category of *musique concrète.*

Most tape-loudspeaker music shares certain basic techniques: the super-imposition of layers of sound through simultaneous recording and dubbing, and the alteration of sound characteristics through the use of electronic filters, reverberation, tape loops (providing endless pattern-repetition), control of intensity, change of tape speed (producing transpositions of register up or down to the limits of equipment response), and chopping and splicing of tape in limitless combinations and juxtapositions, affecting the character of single sounds or whole structures. Sound transformations involving the finest distinctions or the most gradual rates of change may be juxtaposed with the most violent contrasts and the extremes can be mediated by every possible gradation in between.

Some of these procedures, developed and used at Cologne, at other European studios, and at the Columbia University studio founded in 1952, can be bypassed with the R.C.A. Synthesizer, which does away with many "hand" techniques to achieve direct results. Similar advances are envisaged in the planning for the new Stockholm studio; and computer techniques developed at Bell Laboratories and elsewhere, although as yet of limited musical importance, suggest that it may be possible some day for a composer to work directly through computer programming without any tape tampering at all.

None of this, it should be added, implies a music composed by machines.[3] The composer of electronic music works, as the painter always has done, directly with his medium. He has all the advantages of extended resources and controls. He can, if he wishes, realize complexities and subtle transformations, structural forms and detailed relationships, whose limits become—and this is really the new and crucial point—the limits of the ability of the human ear and the human intelligence to perceive them.

The use of electronic media had a very specific importance in Stockhausen's work: it offered him the possibility of creating new forms out of the conception of the serial control of transformation and rate of change.

---

[3] A computer can also be used, of course, to originate musical materials and to put them together. To the extent that this involves unforeseen results, "computer composition" is a chance music (really the only one possible) producing random music within the limitations provided by the programmer. This must not be confused with the general question of electronic means and media.

Stockhausen's earlier instrumental works use material based on values ar-ranged in fixed steps—sometimes conceived in terms of arbitrary and un-idiomatic distinctions. In his electronic music—in particular, in his *Gesang der Jünglinge* of 1956—he could break away from the discreteness imposed by the use of individual instruments and by the tempered scale, and literally break down conventional distinctions between noise and pitch, between clarity and complexity, between the simple statement and the transformed event, between pure electronic and recorded vocal sound, between verbal meaning and abstract sound pattern, between suddenness and gradualness, even between sound and silence. Later, partly under influences coming from the United States, Stockhausen was to discover a way of reinterpreting these principles in terms of "live," performed music; in a way, it was the electronic experience which was decisive. In 1959 Stockhausen wrote a tape piece which is entirely structured on great continuous sliding transformations of every possible aspect—every dimen-sion or, to use the term in vogue, "parameter"—of musical sound. This work, *Kontakte*, also exists in a version with two piano and percussion performers, in which even the gap between purely electronically produced and live sound is closed.

The Columbia University electronic studio, founded by Otto Luening (b. 1900) and Vladimir Ussachevsky (b. 1911) in 1952, pre-dates every-thing in the field except the first *musique concrète* and some of the first experimental work in Cologne. Luening and Ussachevsky tended from the very first to use live and live-recorded sound in conjunction with tape techniques; they were, after Varèse, the first to explore the now-important relationship of tape and live sounds. Nevertheless, they have shown a preference for adapting new techniques and resources to old patterns. Of the younger composers who have worked at Columbia, Mario Davidovsky (b. 1934), an Argentinian now living in the United States, Bülent Arel (b. 1918), a Turk now returned to his native country, and the former jazz pianist Mel Powell (b. 1923), now director of the recently founded Yale University electronic studio, have worked with the prob-lems of creating new forms out of new and not-so-new electronic mate-rials.

The most important of the numerous (and often ephemeral) elec-tronic studios founded in Europe during the 1950's[4] was the Studio di Fonologia in Milan under the direction of the Italian composers Luciano Berio (b. 1925) and Bruno Maderna (b. 1920). The electronic work of Berio and Maderna—one should also add the name of the Belgian Henri Pousseur (b. 1929)—although originally identified with the serial tech-niques of their instrumental music, was characterized by a close, empirical experimentation with the new material. With a few exceptions—Berio's *Omaggio à Joyce* (1958) and his *Visages*, both examples of a large-scale

[4] Holland, Warsaw, Munich, etc.; by now, some kind of electronic work has been produced in virtually every musically active country.

combination of electronic and vocal sound—most of the Milan studio works have had the character of limited exploratory studies, essays in the discovery and transformation of materials. With the experience of electronic music, the younger European composers turned away from closed twelve-tone conceptions; the next step, the return to instrumental music, was to be accomplished with the abandonment or drastic modification of the old concept of predetermined materials and fixed, closed form.

Bibliography

Milton Babbitt's formulation of twelve-tone structure as a system is scattered in several extremely technical articles in *Perspectives of New Music*, *The Score*, the *Journal of Music Theory*, and the *Musical Quarterly*; perhaps the most accessible expositions are those in *The Score* (December, 1963) and the *Musical Quarterly* (April, 1960; the entire issue later reprinted as "Problems of Modern Music"). There is no similarly comprehensive or systematic material on European serialism; see, however, György Ligeti's explication of Boulez's *Structures* in *Die Reihe*, No. 4.

For *musique concrète*, see *Sept Ans de musique concrète* (Paris, 1954) and the special issue of the *Revue musicale*, No. 236. *Die Reihe*, No. 1, is devoted to electronic music. A brief survey of European and American electronic developments may be found in the author's article in the August, 1964, issue of *High Fidelity*.

14
Anti-Rationality and Aleatory

The appearance of "totally organized," totally rational music and th systematic abandonment of conscious, pre-set composer control wer precisely coincidental in time. John Cage came out of the Ives-Cowel line and his early music is, in some respects, the end rather than the begin ning of a development; it is, like much of Cowell's work of the 1930 and 1940's, concerned with non-tempered sounds, with percussion an with Oriental ideas. Cage's famous prepared piano is a kind of one-ma percussion ensemble (often closely related in sound to the Javanese game lan). A more prophetic idea was the use of phonographic test records t produce a kind of proto-electronic music. Eventually Cage abandoned, no only steady-state pitch phenomena, but also rational control over man spects of the musical event. He used dice,[1] the Chinese *I Ching* chance manual, random plotting on the imperfections of a piece of paper—not o give the performers freedom, but to de-control the conscious manipulation of sound. He produced a pair of tape-collage pieces (among the earliest tape pieces anywhere) as well as his famous *Imaginary Landscape* or twelve radios, random noise assemblages whose subject matter is a fixed time span within which aural objects—any aural objects (including other music) in any combination—may occur, plucked from the real word by random, intentionally irrelevant methods and put in random juxtaposition. Fixed time segments and some kind of graphic, schematic, or diagrammatic notations—newly invented or plotted for each piece—are characteristic of the live performed pieces. These notations are basically programs for activities; they renounce any specific control of actual sound results but merely define the limits of choice, the possible field of activity, and the impossibility of prediction. Scores or parts may be played separately, together, or not at all. Instruments are objects to be acted upon; sounds are a series of unpredictable disturbances and interferences. The graphic representation becomes partly an end in itself, a significant catalyst in an on-going relationship between creator, performer, and listener. Musical performance becomes a kind of existentialist activity in which the notions of "musical composition," of "performance," of communication, and of the "work of art" itself are destroyed or drastically altered; in which the real, determined world and the unreal, accidental world of "art" merge; in which the listener becomes directly involved in an activity in which the old distinctions and relationships are meaningless. Ultimately there need be no activity at all—only an open piano and the contemplation of *4'33"* of nothing at all. Cage's famous silent piece, the classic and pure piece of non-music (1954) may be taken as a frame for the natural sounds of life, a segment of time isolated and defined in order to trap, for a moment, the experience of the haphazard, "real" world. Or it may be taken as the zero point of perception where total randomness and aleatory meet total determinism and unity in the literal experience of nothing.

Cage is not perhaps to be considered as a creator in the ordinary sense —but then he has done a great deal to change that "ordinary sense." He has been and remains one of the most influential figures in avant-garde arts since the war, and aspects of his work have generated whole esthetics of graphic notation; of performance as gesture; of chance, choice, and changes; of "neo-realist" use of accidental or chosen sound objects from the exterior world. Electronic music suddenly seemed to make the whole

[1] *Alea*, Latin for dice, is the root of the word "aleatory," currently (and loosely) used to describe various kinds of music in which chance elements, randomness, and indeterminacy figure in the "realization" in performance. Another adjectival form is "aleatoric"; this is decried by some critics on the grounds that "aleatory" is already an adjective related to the French *aléatoire* meaning "chancy" or "risky." As usual, usage outruns etymology.

question of perfect order and rationality in performed music irrelevant
It is in the nature of human activity that a precise action can never be re
peated and that no event can ever recur; it seemed logical, particularly t
the European dialectic mind, that irrationality and randomness shoul
be built in as qualifications for the construction of a new instrumenta
and performed music. Actually, of course, irrationality and randomnes
are no more the essence of the human condition than is man's capacity t
impose or conceptualize order in the external world. When a mathe
matician wants true randomness he turns to the machine; there is at leas
one example of a composer, Yannis Xenakis (b. 1922), a Greek now livin
in Paris, who has used computer and related techniques to generate ran
dom statistical patterns—bunches of unpredictable events sprayed over
given field—which are subsequently translated into instrumental soun
values.

An obvious corollary to the de-rationalization of composer contro
was the increased importance given to the performer's role in determinin
the details or the actual shape of a conception in performance. Already i
the early 1950's, a number of composers—Earle Brown (b. 1926), Morto
Feldman (b. 1926), Christian Wolff (b. 1934), comprising a New Yor
school of "action music" close to but distinct from Cage—began to ope
up spaces within which multiple possibilities could be realized at th
moment of execution. New notations were invented for these purposes
not only to indicate graphically the limitations of the space within whic
the performer could operate but also to re-engage the interpreter in a kin
of dialectic vis-à-vis the score. The notations generally have exactly th
opposite significance from the scientific, graphic indications which the
often externally resemble. Scientific notations are ways of representin
the precise course of observed events, generally on a continuum. Mos
of the musical graphics are, on the contrary, only generalized guide
intended merely to outline or suggest to the performers the areas in whic
choice and chance are permitted to operate. Thus Feldman will, withir
a typically soft and spare arrangement of sound events, indicate genera
areas of attack, pitch, or register, the exact choice being left to the per
former; the sound events are carefully isolated and disassociated from
one another. Intentional disassociation—statement without relationship
evolution, or process—is a fundamental, underlying idea. Brown's *Decem
ber 1952* is a series of horizontal and vertical black rectangles inked on
white sheet, indicating only certain very general co-ordinates; withir
these, all choices are possible and equally valid. It is important not to con
fuse this music with improvisation; there is no question here of perform
ance tradition or spontaneous invention within some given pattern bu
only controlled choice situations in which any rational basis for decisior
has been intentionally removed or minimized.

These techniques of performer choice and of automatic chanc
mechanisms were also applied to the actual sequence of events in a per

formance and, thus, to larger "structure." By the application of an inexhaustible series of devices—shuffling pages, selecting fragments, performers interacting with one another, performers totally ignoring one another, live performance pitted against tape, and so forth—a conception can be designed that will, on each reading, result in a new juxtaposition of the parts. In theory, there will be some constant from one performance to the next that, in some sense, defines a particular conception throughout all its transformations, but in many cases, this constant would seem to be only the program for action itself.

Cage's earlier chance compositions tend to be fixed, principally in some kind of determined time span (details open, over-all space closed); after Cowell, Brown seems to have been the first to propose open form (details fixed; sequence variable). Later on, Cage also adopted the notion of multi-directional structures, applying this to diagrammatic programs of action; a work like his *Piano Concert* consists of a piano part, whose elements can be played in any order desired, and an orchestral part, to be realized by any number of players (including none) on any number of instruments, playing parts made up of pages of which any number may be played (including none), with or without other instruments. Beyond the free-will, existentialist music of chance and changes, Cage moved on into a vaster area of activity and gesture. He attached contact microphones to instruments and scratched record pick-ups and mike heads, clogging the lines of amplified communication with violent, random electronic "distortion"; he sent electronic feedback whirling through speaker systems and across the thresholds of perception and pain; he smoked cigarettes and swallowed water, contact mike at the throat, volume at full blast. Typically, he has left the explanation of complex and multiplying noise levels and indeterminacies to others and has moved logically onwards (he has always been more of a dialectician than his interest in Oriental ideas would lead one to believe) to a kind of ritual theatre in which the act of performance becomes a way of drawing together meaningless and unordered bits of real life. *Indeterminacy: New Aspect of Form in Instrumental and Electronic Music* is, in spite of its grand title, a set of ninety funny stories—accompanied, interrupted, or blotted out by piano and electronic activities taken from the *Piano Concert*—slowly recited or gabbled through to make each story fit a one-minute space. His *Theater Piece* is a big collage of action and gesture indeterminately organized in a determinate time space.

A great deal of this is defined in a purely negative way: by the exclusion of possibility or by a simple reversal of traditional premises. Instead of organizing sounds in relationship to one another, Feldman creates a sound content whose elements are intentionally unrelated and disassociated. Instead of a definable work of art, there are "compositions" which consist of a set of activities regulated by delineations of limitation, with an intentional disassociation between the nature of the activity and its possible results in sound. Instead of being conceived as sound, performances are based on visual definitions, programs of activity, and ideas of non-sound or silence. Instead of defining time, the compositions are themselves defined by the random passage of time extending to indeterminate or possibly infinite length. Instead of a music of definable identity, we have conceptions whose essence is lack of identity. There are activities by La Monte Young (b. 1935) which consist of directions like "Hold this for a long time" or "Prepare any piece and play it." There are "compositions" which direct performers to sit on the stage and look at the audience, to burn musical instruments or to sit in cars, blow horns, and flash lights. We proceed in short, inevitable steps from long sets of meaningless directions for meaningless and useless "existentialist" actions to a kind of "neo-realist" Theatre of Aimless Activity (as opposed to the "theatre of the absurd") and then to "Happenings" and perhaps on to meaningless, useless real life.

The influence of all these kinds of activities has been very great in all the arts (more importantly outside of music, perhaps) in the United States, Europe, and even the Far East.[2] This influence has ranged from the simple use of random noise techniques and chance procedures to various projects for a "neo-realist" theater of gesture and object. Stockhausen has used some kind of aleatory or open-form procedure in every one of his works since his *Klavierstücke XI* of 1956 (made up of short piano segments which can be put together in different ways) and *Zyklus* of 1957 (a percussion piece written in a graphic notation and open for realization on a simple ground plan). Virtually all European avant-garde music of the last few years has been affected in some way. Mauricio Kagel (b. 1931), an Argentinian now living in Germany, has been specifically involved with the character of performance as gesture and activity. Others, including a number of young Germans and an Italian group working in an area close to "pop art," have used actual pre-existing sound objects as well as sets of activities and gestures for the materials of paste-up neo-realist collages. Stockhausen himself has written a Cage-like (but structured) theatre piece—*Originale*—and there has been a spate of random gestural-theatre ventures of one sort or another. In the United States, "action" activity groups like "Fluxus" in New York and exponents of a kind of mobile, kinetic music like the "Once" group in Michigan are committed to the idea of activity—musical, meaningless or otherwise—as a way of life.

[2] A curious return of a compliment, since Cage and the "New York School" have appropriated ideas from the Orient. Japanese (and also Korean) composers have participated actively in musical developments of recent years. The best known of the Japanese Cage-ians is Toshiro Ichiyanagi. Many of the other Japanese, the Matsudairas, father and son, Toru Takemitsu, Toshiro Mayuzumi, and Kazuo Fukushima, as well as the Korean Isang Yun, have tended towards an adaptation of European serialism, tempered by Oriental elements and, increasingly, chance, indeterminate, open-form, or even gestural materials derived from the "New York School."

Bibliography

There is no clearly distinguishable line between Cage's writings about his works and the works themselves: see his articles in *Die Reihe*, Nos. 3 and 4, and *The Score* (July, 1955); his introduction to the Folkways record album *Indeterminacy;* and a number of his essays, including the text portions of works like *45′ for a Speaker* and *Indeterminacy: New Aspect of Form in Instrumental and Electronic Music*, in the book titled *Silence* (Wesleyan University Press, 1961).

On the "Fluxus" group and related phenomena, there are a number of privately printed collections of events, proposals, and other matter; the best-known is the anthology (called *Anthology*) put together by La Monte Young and George Brecht.

For European aleatory material, see the later issues of *Die Reihe* and the *Darmstädter Beitrage*. Boulez's "Alea," originally presented at Darmstadt in 1957 as a proposal for a new music, is printed in English translation in the Fall–Winter, 1964, issue of *Perspectives of New Music;* the Fall–Winter, 1965, issue includes "Indeterminacy: Some Considerations," by Roger Reynolds, formerly of the "Once" group.

15
The New Performed Music

The serial and chance musics of the early 1950's, apparently contradictory, shared certain premises: all of this music was deductive, experimental in a strict sense. There are a limited number of pre-compositional hypotheses—negatively defined by a rigorous exclusion of possibility—and the music is, so to speak, deduced from the unique set of premises. The premises are simple and limited; the deductions are thorough, extreme, and encompassing—they are, in a sense, equivalent to the piece.

Taken in sum, this music affirmed (or perhaps only reaffirmed) the principle that each conception had to establish its own unique premises—the actual content of a work and the relationships (including non-relationships) of its parts as they unfold, as they are acted upon, interact, or intersect in time, are defined uniquely by each work as its particular structure. The total effect was to redefine every aspect of the creative and interpretive act and to make the total range of experience itself (including the new experiences of form) the natural subject matter of the new music. The new techniques of total control, of chance, and, especially, of magnetic tape, made this totality more than just a theoretical possibility. Any experience is now available; its significance can only depend on its use. This totality of experience is coming to form, not merely a fund of materials and processes, but the context out of which each new work grows. The range of possibility is represented by a slice of it—a cross-grain cut, so to speak—organized, not through pre-compositional assumptions, but through an act of mediating extremes, the premises and conditions of which must be re-established by each work and even each performance of each work. It is the actual range of perception and comprehension that is involved, and the new music is "about" the quality and nature of heightened experience, perception, thought, and understanding, communicated throughout the range of human capacities. There is here a new totality of forms and psychological validities which come out of a universalized experience but which are re-established in particular by each work.

The best recent music then is inductive instead of deductive, comprehensive instead of exclusive, analytic, so to speak, instead of synthetic. It deals with: (1) the conditions of the live performance situation interpreted in terms of control (the tension growing out of the necessity to put the right finger in the right place at the right time) interacting with freedom (the flexibility of actions whose precise value is determined only at the moment of performance); (2) an interaction between composer and performer as well as between performers; (3) an interaction between live and recorded (or live and live-amplified) sound projected in physical space; (4) improvisatory and controlled virtuosity set at the limits of performer possibility; (5) the exploration of the limits of form perception. It, further, comes out of the relationships, juxtapositions, and oppositions of such aspects of experience as strictness and freedom, rational control and irrationality, fixed detail and improvisation, total unity and open form, symmetry and asymmetry, periodicity and a-periodicity, extreme register and extreme dynamic, maximum motion and utter stasis, high and low tension, thinness and density, complexity and simplicity, confusion and clarity, intelligibility and incomprehensibility, pitch and noise, sound and silence, expressive-and-isolated-detail and big-line-and-form. This is no longer a music of fixed goals but of transformations which take place in every dimension and throughout the range of perception. These transformations become ways of acting, experiencing, and relating action and experience (i.e., of knowing), and they can actually alter, extend, and redefine the quality and limits of our ability to perceive and comprehend.

In Europe, some change of direction could already be seen in the mid-1950's: Luigi Nono's *Il Canto sospeso* (1955–1956), with its use of multilayered vocal-choral sound; Stockhausen's *Zeitmasse* (1956) for wind quintet, with its alternation of controlled and flexible situations (loosening of vertical ties in parts played individually "as fast as possible" or "as slow as possible"); Pierre Boulez's *Le Marteau sans maître* (1955), which begins to substitute a complex poetic form for a merely serial one. Change is evident in Milton Babbitt's *All Set, Vision and Prayer,* and *Philomel,* works which, although they remain faithful to a vision of total rationality and control, also relate to the character of the live performance situation and the virtuosity of the performer.

The development of this "new virtuosity" can be traced in the work of Elliott Carter (b. 1908), a pupil of Nadia Boulanger whose initial view was neo-classical and, in great part, concerned with vocal music. At the end of the 1940's and early in the 1950's, Carter began to expand his vocabulary in the direction of a non-twelve-tone instrumental chromaticism. Works like the intense first String Quartet (1951), based on long contrapuntal lines, and the more decorative and elegant Sonata for flute, oboe, cello, and harpsichord (1953), with its new element of ornamental virtuosity, grow out of the interaction of complex parts; the *Eight Etudes and a Fantasy* for woodwind quartet (1952) constitute a set of close-up studies of simple and very precisely defined material; the most remarkable is a study on a single pitch. By the *Variations for Orchestra* of 1955 and the second String Quartet of 1959, Carter had achieved an identification of the material, the performing situation, and the individualization of the players through a form which is non-serial yet controlled, flexible and "invented" yet completely organic. In the second String Quartet, the four players are separated in physical space and completely individualized in their musical way of speaking; the parts are related by a common virtuosity—a kind of highly ornamented fantasy style in which the "embellishments" and colors are not merely decorative but organic and essential— and yet each has distinct characteristics of pitch, rhythm, and dynamic. The totality of the piece is a confluence of divergent currents which retain their identity while remaining essential parts of the larger flow. In the *Double Concerto* for piano and harpsichord of 1960–1961, the two solo instruments are set off against one another, each with its own small ensemble of winds and strings, plus a huge battery of percussion which literally frames the piece in highly articulated noise. The pitch content of the piece emerges from and eventually returns to a more undifferentiated state of percussion "noise," and these transitions are, so to speak, mediated by the soloists who perform on what are, in effect, pitched percussion instruments. The same integrated opposition which exists between pitch and noise on one level operates, on another plane, between interval pattern and rhythm; and these in turn generate a big structure of changing "modulating" tempos. Again, as in the second String Quartet, the parts are distinguished by complementary pitch and rhythmic content. The total impression becomes that of a sum of disparate elements—a sum of rhythms for example, which generates a higher-level pulse which ultimately deter-mines the over-all motion. The rhythmic groupings and phrase articula-tions, taken through wide changes of register and timbre, carry out the association of pitch, texture, and rhythm; just as there is a sum of rhythms, there is a sum of textures, lines, and harmonic conglomerations which inte-grates highly differentiated material and derives a new and expressive form from them.

There is a relationship between Carter's conception of a music which results from the complex intersection of independent parts and the recent music of Stefan Wolpe (b. 1902)—*In Two Parts* for flute and piano, *In Two Parts* for six players, *Piece for Two Instrumental Units*—which takes shape from the constant interplay of oppositions of clarity and complexity, simplicity and density, careful articulation and great freedom. Wolpe, like Varèse, was born and trained in Europe, but his mature work is identified with the American scene; the striking individuality of his ideas, his conception of an ordered freedom, and his interest in organic forms place him in the tradition of American individualism. Wolpe's forms, like Varèse's, accumulate as great static objects, but the ideas and the small-range motion are full of revolving, intense motion. Works like the flute and piano piece are built on tiny, cell-like structures which retain their essential, immovable identity through every kind of registral, rhythmic, dynamic, and color shift; the formal result is a kind of accumulation of potential energies which twist, turn, combine and recombine, destroy and reconstruct an apparently unyielding material.

The concept of cumulative form, already present in the work of composers like Varèse and Wolpe, is particularly significant in the music of younger composers like Chou Wen-chung (b. 1923, Chinese-American pupil of Varèse) and Ralph Shapey (b. 1921). Shapey's music—*Discourse* for flute, clarinet, violin, and piano of 1960–1961 can serve as a typical example—uses large, contrasting, blocklike ideas set forth in broad planes and constantly returning in great overlapping phased cycles. Within a static structure of balanced, inflexible, and immobile units, there is a kind of internal play of energies resulting from the continuous redefinition of a fixed material which remains set in a constant state of tension. This music, like that of Wolpe and of a number of younger composers—the String Quartet of Billy Jim Layton (b. 1924) is an excellent example—suggests—in the context of live performance realized in real, directional time—a new significance for forms which use symmetry, repetition, and periodicity as well as asymmetry, non-repetition and a-periodicity.

A great deal of new music in both Europe and the United States is closely associated with an enormous expansion of the role and character of instrumental techniques and, indeed, with the very personalities, musi-cal and artistic, of the performers themselves. Cage's work has been closely identified with the realization of the pianist David Tudor; similarly, works of Stockhausen have inevitably taken their actual, known shape through the "interpretations" (the old term has particular relevance here) of pianists like Paul Jacobs and Frederick Rzewski or percussionists like Christoff Caskel and Max Neuhaus. The influence of the style and ability of performers like the flutist Severino Gazzelloni and the sopranos Bethany Beardslee and Cathy Berberian in the character and realization of the new music written for them has been considerable. A composer like Earle Brown has evolved a very characteristic performance music in which a kind of controlled improvisatory freedom is arrived at through the interaction of the musicians on the spot. Works like *Available Forms 1* and *2* (1961–1962; for chamber ensemble and orchestra respectively) are based on neither aleatory nor traditional improvisational procedures (which use fixed or periodic forms with improvised detail); they are made up of fixed details which can be "improvised" into a form. The performers make their decisions by reacting, within a specified technique, to each other as well as to the flexible character of the music at hand. In *Available Forms 2*, a normal orchestra in normal seating arrangement is divided into two intermeshed groups, each of which responds to the cues of an independent conductor; each conductor chooses material at the given moment by responding to the immediate situation and to the choices of his confrère. As with any improvisational material, the results can be extremely variable depending on, among other things, the skill and sensitivity of the performers; when everything is working well, there is a sense of lively, organized spontaneity, a kind of controlled incoherence of great vitality, and, from time to time, a real impression of "discovered" form arising from the interaction of an effectively conceived musical action and gesture. Example 15-1 shows three out of five possible "events" on a page of score for one of the two orchestras of *Available Forms 2*. The conductor of each orchestra successively selects various events during the course of the performance and indicates his choices to the musicians by holding up the fingers of one hand.

The only important living tradition of improvisation in Western music is, of course, jazz, and any comprehensive view of music in the twentieth century ought to take into account its development (still imperfectly understood) from origins in handed-down harmonic, rhythmic, and instrumental tradition to the complex, creative freedom of its modern forms. Here it must suffice to say that, just as modern "concert" music is approaching the conditions of jazz—in improvisatory freedom, instrumental virtuosity, and so forth—so has modern jazz been approaching the conditions of avant-garde music—in chromaticism, serial technique, open or on-going form. Gunther Schuller (b. 1925), himself a performer and conductor in both fields, has combined the techniques of modern jazz improvisation with the controlled intellectual conceptions of a twelve-tone style. Schuller, who coined the term "third stream" for this intersection of traditions, has carried this conception of the interaction of fixed and free over into his written-out twelve-tone music, which grows out of a spon-

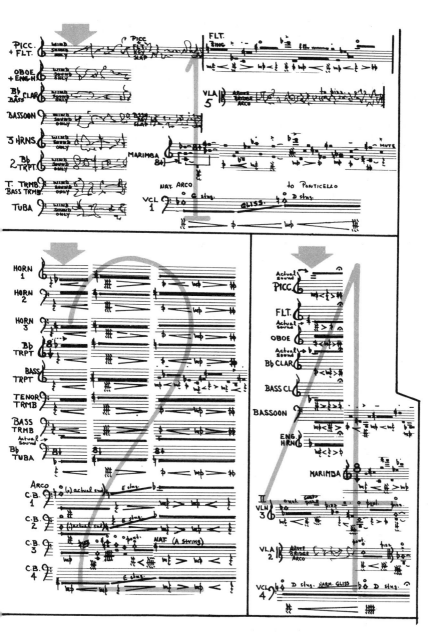

EXAMPLE 15-1. Brown, *Available Forms 2;* excerpt from *Orchestra 1* score.
Quoted by permission of Associated Music Publishers, Inc.

taneous and idiomatic instrumental invention that often opens up to allow for the image, if not the actual substance, of improvisation. The compositions of "third-stream" composers like Schuller, William Smith, John Eaton, Larry Austin, and Peter Phillips, and the music of jazzmen like Ornette Coleman, John Coltrane, Jimmy Giuffre, Lalo Schifrin, Cecil Taylor, John Lewis and others can be distinguished from each other in approach, but the identification with the controlled richness of a complex, modern virtuoso performing style is basic and common to all. The free, extreme explorations of the younger men—Albert Ayler, Bill Dixon, Sun Ra, Giuseppi Logan—shake off the conventional idea of jazz sound entirely and approach the conditions of the most "advanced" experimental work; their music relates to jazz only in its impromptu, intuitive, ecstatic qualities.

There have been a number of attempts to create non-jazz improvisation styles and techniques, many of them centered in California. A great deal of this activity has been in the San Francisco area, where the composer Robert Erickson has been working out new techniques with performing musicians both in purely improvisational situations and in written scores which incorporate some of these ideas. A number of younger composers in the area—Austin, Pauline Oliveros, Morton Subotnick, and Loren Rush —have similarly been working with new performance-practice notions.

Perhaps the first and best-known work in this field was that of Lukas Foss (b. 1922), who founded his Improvisational Chamber Ensemble in Los Angeles in the late 1950's. Foss's idea was—in the absence of a performing tradition—to invent the conditions (basically, the limitations) within which a new kind of improvisation could take place. The importance of the Ensemble was not so much the demonstration of the possibilities of spontaneity and "discovered form" as the corroboration of a new vitality in creative performance based on the character of the instruments and the skill and personality of the players.[1] Foss became musical director of the Buffalo Symphony, and the activity of the Ensemble has lapsed, although its founder has been pursuing related ideas in a performance ensemble project in Buffalo and in his own written-out music as well. His *Time Cycle* (1960) in its various versions (some of which can include actual improvisation) and, especially, his *Echoi* of 1963, have the character of free and exceptionally successful improvisations; the forms are controlled, yet they give the impression of growing out of the character of the detail which is, in turn, an outgrowth of a genial conception of the pleasures and possibilities of a live and lively performance situation.

Echoi and, even more notably, recent works of Carter and Wolpe, relate closely to the work of younger American composers which comes out of the activity of performance as expressed through tensions between performers, materials, and score. Thus, the music of Charles Wuorinen

---

[1] The work of the Ensemble closely followed Foss' own evolution from "neo-classicism" to serialism and aleatory.

(b. 1938), which has its point of origin in the composer's own remarkable technique as pianist (a technique which includes, besides fistfuls of notes articulated in the usual way, the brushing and slamming of the keys with fingers, palm and fist; plunking, hitting, and scratching the strings directly inside the piano; etc.), develops its expressive structure out of a series of on-going oppositions between forward thrust and tense immobility, violent energy and violent calm, and so forth. Similarly, a work like the *Chamber Variations* of Wuorinen's colleague at Columbia University, the flutist Harvey Sollberger, grows initially out of an extraordinary virtuoso instrumental technique, characterized by a tension of contrasts and the unified opposition of extremes, tightly controlled at first, then decontrolled, ultimately, in every dimension and with extreme precision. (So many of the younger American composers are themselves expert instrumentalists, or conductors, that one can almost speak of a "school" of performer-composers and of a performance-practice music.) Salvatore Martirano's *0, 0, 0, 0, That Shakespeherian Rag*, a setting of Shakespeare for chorus and ensemble, extends the idea of solo virtuosity into a big choral conception with vocal writing (informed by the character of the texts) built on singing, speaking, trilling, hissing, whispering, and shouting; the instrumental frame (informed by a virtuoso performing technique evolved at a point close to jazz) is at once contradictory and essential, equally free and equally planned in a structure which is both controlled and dramatic. The present author's *The Owl and the Cuckoo*, also a setting of Shakespeare for voice and ensemble, is a confluence of virtuoso solo parts, framed in the sound of solo voice and guitar, deriving its form from a parallel double structure based on the opposition of poetic images and sound values in the text and the use of closed, controlled performance techniques (i.e. precisely notated sung and played pitched music) and ones that are freer or less carefully defined (i.e., cadenzas, bird-song vocalises, unusual instrumental sounds including percussive raps and clicks on pitched instruments). A setting from John Ashbery's *The Tennis Court Oath*, also by the author, provides a further extension of the concept of performed music by the use of microphones and loud-speakers: a separate score and a group of "technician-performers" control the direction and intensity of the amplified sound of the ensemble of singers and instrumentalists—the live performers thus interact, not only with each other, but with the amplified image of their own playing and singing as it moves out, around, and back through a series of loudspeakers placed around the hall.

The "new virtuosity" is no longer mere embellishment but part of the organic conception of the musical substance itself. A unified set of actions and gestures functions as a source of thematic ideas which form relationships, oppositions, and interactions in the performance situation: between performer and score, between real (i.e. clock) time and psychological time; between fixed units of measure and open cadenza; between control and complex precision on the one hand and the open play of color and virtuosity on the other; between the idea of the uniqueness of the individual performer (in character, in material, even in space) and the concept of a coherent unity; between the requirements of perceptible form and new concepts of idea, activity, and substance extended in every direction and in every dimension to the most extreme limits.

After the middle 1950's, as we have suggested, the character of avant-garde European music began to change drastically; the use of totally controlled serialism growing out of the identity of the isolated musical event gave way to a new material based on transformations of densities, colors and textures; on the "statistical" (i.e. controlled chance) arrangement of events; on multiple, open, or "chance" forms. The systematic development and application of such ideas in European music is largely due to Stockhausen. Stockhausen argued for the controlled use of multiple realization as a new conception of performed music, and he argued that such new techniques were in themselves new forms; a work like his *Momente* (1958) is conceived as a complete set of possible realizations for what he designates as the "Moment" form—the scheme, so to speak, for an infinite number of possible actual realizations. In effect, the basis of these new forms—one to a piece, with Stockhausen—is an extension of the concept of serialization into every dimension of the musical conception; even, for example, the amount and quality of specific compositional control over the performers is arranged on a serial scale of values ranging from total notated control to extreme variability. Performer action may be designated by graphic notations that delimit fields of wide or limited choice, elaborate and loose densities of note spattering or very closely unified sound structures, with transformations through all possible values in between. Similarly, Stockhausen began to use a basic material which ranges away from pitch towards a complex use of "noise"—that is, patterns of unfixed or random frequency content—and away from all types of simple, steady-states to complex superimpositions of oscillating patterns. He serialized density and complexity themselves; he serialized periodicity (that is, cyclical and repeated structures) and a-periodicity (or asymmetrical and non-repetitive structures); he serialized the concept of transformation and change, the disposition of sounds in physical space, and the perception of clarity and complexity, comprehensibility and confusion; he serialized ways of perceiving; and he serialized the construction of time and the ways of acting—of "performing"—in time. Out of all this, Stockhausen derived a characteristic notion of form: the unique set of propositions in each piece which relate these various kinds of serialized activity. Beginning with *Zeitmasse* and continuing with *Klavierstücke XI, Zyklus, Refrain* for three keyboard-percussion players, the theatre piece *Originale, Gruppen* for three orchestras, *Momente* for chorus, keyboard, percussion, and brass instruments, and *Carré* for four choruses and four instrumental ensembles, each conception is a specific representation of very carefully defined formal, serial techniques, each developed uniquely for the particular conception. Thus, *Momente* is based on an enormous range of performing activities including all kinds of playing, banging, singing, speaking, hand-clapping, feet-shuffling, whispering, and babbling, all arranged in varying degrees of control and randomness, clusters and isolated tones, densities and simplicities, clarities and confusions—even the communication of the texts (which must be translated into the language of the local country) is serialized with regard to comprehensibility. All of this material is arranged into a series of events or "moments"—not isolated sounds but complex occurrences of a given duration—which, by an arbitrary arrangement of the pages of the scores and parts, may be placed in any order. Finally, even any given sequence of these events or "moments" is further complicated by a system of interpolations—insertions or "tropes," one might say—in which material from certain events may be anticipated or recalled during the performance of others.

In one sense, all of Stockhausen's work has been based on a series (in the informal as well as specific sense) of propositions about sound material and ways of acting on this material—not so much about form as about ways of forming. Thus, the microphone and amplification techniques in his recent work are used, not, as in recent American works, to project a faithful or distorted image set off in space against live sound, but to extend and project the relatively fixed and discrete actions and events of a live performance onto a broader continuum in which every sound possibility is extendable and capable of being merged into any other sound possibility. *Microphonie I* (1964) is a work for a single tam-tam set in motion by four performers in every conceivable way; two of the players hold microphones which are brought towards and away from the vibrating gong or even actually put into contact with and rubbed against the instrument itself; these amplified vibrations are further taken up by performer-technicians who transmit them to a pair of loudspeakers under all kinds of electronic-filter transformations. The piece is built—like all of Stockhausen's works—directly out of its techniques, out of its ways of forming, of making, and of acting on its materials. Stockhausen has synthesized and systematized—and occasionally created—technique with the ultimate aim of regulating all possible ways of acting on all possible materials. That regulation, that conception of form—or, more exactly, of "forming"—is at the heart of all of his conceptions.

Similar ideas have come to dominate the work of a great number of Central European avant-garde composers (often under the direct influence of Stockhausen): the Swede Bo Nilsson (b. 1934), one of the first to serialize open form and chance techniques and to use microphones; the Hungarian György Ligeti (b. 1923), who has worked with a subject matter made largely out of sliding, shifting densities and colors; the Belgian Henri Pousseur (b. 1929), who has been concerned, at least in a theoretical way, with a kind of serial integration of ideas like repetition (periodicity) and even historical material from the outcast tonal past; the Italian Franco Evangelisti (b. 1926), who has worked with graphic techniques and the consequences of certain systems of transformation and randomization; the Polish-Israeli-Austrian composer, Roman Haubenstock-Ramati (b. 1919), and the Austrian Friedrich Cerha (b. 1926), with their clusters and densities of sound, twisting and turning in open, spatial arrangements. With exceptions—some of the works of Pousseur (more as a theoretician perhaps), the gestural indeterminacies of Kagel—much of this is dominated by the figure of Stockhausen, as a creator and as a source, transmitter, and codifier of new ideas.

It is an odd fact of recent history that the first important European manifestations of twelve-tone and serial technique developed in countries which had previously been the most hostile to these ideas: France and Italy. In a special and remarkable way, the twelve-tone idea had a very particular appeal for a certain kind of French rationalism which, rather than imposing a total vision of order on the world (German style), seeks to rationalize the relationship of man to his experience of the world. Pierre Boulez (b. 1925), a pupil of Messiaen, began as a twelve-tone *enfant terrible* and became, for a brief moment, a totally organized, totally serial super-rationalist. The early twelve-tone works of the late 1940's—the *Second Piano Sonata* (1948), the *Sonatine* for flute and piano (1950), the *Livre* for string quartet (1949)—find their rationale, not only in the Viennese operations of an expressive twelve-tone method, but in the relationship of this method to a virtuoso content built on timbre, texture, dynamic accent and an on-going form. Later, with *Polyphonie X* for 18 instruments (1951) and the first book of *Structures* for two pianos (1951–1952), Boulez committed himself to a completely systematic and predetermined conception of a total material. But these works raise more problems than they solve. *Structures I* is the classical monument of totally organized serial technique in the European avant-garde music of the early 1950's, but its method of making relationships is at once too easy, too numerological, and too irrelevant to the real issues of organic form to be convincing. (A second book, written later, is an intentional antithesis to the closed, classical, uni-directional rationality of the first). In general, the authority *Structures I* possesses seems to stem from Boulez's own considerable personal authority as a pianist and performing musician.

Le Marteau sans maître (1954) is, by contrast, one of the first avant-garde European works to escape the narrow confines of a strictly interpreted serialism; in some ways a continuation of Boulez's earlier twelve-tone music, it also marked a new development of ideas descended from the "new" music of the first decades of the century, now informed by a generalized serial technique and a newly rationalized conception of form whose aim is the effective control of fluctuating masses, colors, densities, and intensities of sound. After *Le Marteau*, Boulez extended these conceptions in still other directions—notably in the use of performer choice and multi-directional forms. But *Le Marteau*, a group of vocal settings surrounded by instrumental "commentaries," already contains the basic patterns and many of the modes of thought which became dominant in Boulez's later works: the Third Piano Sonata, *Pli selon pli* (*Portrait de Mallarmé*) for voice and orchestra, and *Doubles* for orchestra (all composed over a period of years beginning in the late 1950's). These works are by no means the free, improvisatory, post-serial fantasies they have sometimes been made out to be. They all contain related but free-standing sections or movements, each based on independent and preconceived forms or formal plans of action. The sections were written and often performed separately as a series of steps in a "work-in-progress" conception (even the present form of *Le Marteau* is a revision dating from 1957; several sections of *Pli selon pli* were rewritten after being composed and performed separately; *Doubles*, already reworked, is a movement from a projected larger work). The intentionally ambiguous, open relationship of the parts to the total scheme is built into the conception; the whole might be compared to a system of planetary bodies discovered, one by one, to be moving around a center of gravity according to fixed relationships yet in a multitude of different actual juxtapositions. The forms themselves originate in a conception of the relationship of the composer to his material, to the world of experience, and to the act of creative communication. These modes of creative thought, often constructed on very specific literary, poetic, or psychological premises, are conceived as ways of acting on a vast and pliable material which is poetic, even, in a sense, discursive, but never really narrative or directional in character. After *Le Marteau* (which is still a series of closed and fixed shapes), Boulez developed ideas of embellishing and of moving on, around, and through a chosen material as revealed in the act of performance. Actually the compositional process seems to be exactly the reverse: that of imagining a concrete and idiomatic material which will function as the poetic realization in time, of a preconceived plan of action.

Unlike most of the European avant-garde composers, Boulez was involved with electronic music only very briefly (and unsuccessfully), and he has always been engaged—as a pianist and, particularly, as a conductor—with the activity of music as a performing art. An involvement with the physical, tangible, even sensuous qualities of the musical material and with the poetic and psychological significance of the activity of producing it has, aside from his brief encounter with strict serialism, given Boulez's music a distinct character within the general flow of new ideas in Europe. The point is that the forms are preconceived and rationalized but they never uniquely generate or predetermine the character of the material; rather they seek to reveal themselves through the quality, fantasy, and imaginative rightness of the ideas. Hence, the impulse—rare among avant-garde composers—to revise and rewrite, to seek the clearest, the richest, the most meaningful realization of the conception. The forms may be open and flexible, but they do not rest on the operations of a chance, statistical, or even an improvisatory method; instead, they seek to reveal the multiple possibilities—the poetic facets so to speak—of the creative imagination. Boulez is very much involved with the significance and impact of personal statement, of the expressive act as arising out of an invented and seemingly open and flexible material which is, however, actually realizing and revealing a hard strategy underneath, a plan which is in itself a rational, poetic realization of a new relationship between the acts of creating, performing, and experiencing a work of art.

Few of the younger French composers have emerged with any clear force of personality from under the influence of Boulez; perhaps André Boucourechliev (b. 1925) and Gilbert Amy (b. 1936) stand out as the most talented and independent. Paris is, however, the home of one of the most individual and certainly the most isolated of the important European avant-gardists: Yannis Xenakis. Xenakis worked for twelve years with the architect Le Corbusier and studied music with Messiaen as well. Beginning with the *Metastasis* of 1953–1954 he began to apply mathematical probability theory to the composition of music. In essence, *Metastasis* and, in varying ways, *Pithoprakta* of 1955–1956 and *Acchoripsis* of 1956–1957 are orchestral ensembles built on sliding, shifting masses and densities whose definition is derived by a "statistical" probability method. Later works—*ST/10–1,080262* of 1962, *Eonta* for piano and brass of 1963, *Strategy* for two orchestras of 1964—extend this conception of the rationalization of the irrational in all domains through the use of electronic computers. With Xenakis, the use of these techniques has nothing to do with any kind of "automatization" of the creative process; the end is always the search for new materials and new forms. Esthetically, the music is big in scale, violent in density and intensity of character, and strongly involved in an idea of the re-creation of the meaning of the act of performance. *Strategy* is a piece for two orchestras and two conductors who literally compete with one another in an attempt to realize a given set of preconditions. Xenakis always defines his conditions precompositionally and in the strictest terms—even when he is dealing with so-called irrationalities (if Cage's is "music of the absurd," this is "music of the surd"). For better or for worse, the ultimate reality of the music (even when miscalculated from a psychological point of view) is to be found in the solution—the engagement with the performing material—as realized on real instruments in real time.

A close involvement with a new and wide-ranging material and an interest in psychological or dramatic form arising out of the character of musical performance and communication is typical of a number of avant-garde European composers, most notably the Italians and Poles. At least three of the younger Italian avant-gardists, Nono, Maderna, and Berio, were first identified with the Central European twelve-tone serial notions of the early 1950's; all of them have worked with electronic techniques;

and all of them have since become closely involved in the projection of poetic, dramatic, or even specifically philosophical-verbal ideas through the medium of a new performed music. In the case of Luigi Nono (b. 1924), these ideas have a specifically social orientation; in the contemporary non-literary arts, Nono remains a rare example of an artist with a strong commitment to relate artistic revolution with the social revolution of our time. The artistic significance of the esthetic point of view is debatable. A work like his opera *Intolleranza* (1960) is a curious hodgepodge of contradictory notions; *La Fabbrica illuminata* (1964), a kind of Orwellian anti-capitalist, anti-Stalinist sound-study of the factory of the future, gains strength from its dramatic, impressive tape babble of voices but is nearly destroyed by its climactic, agonized cry, "factory as concentration camp." The problem is crucial for Nono, and not only because of his views of the social value and impact of avant-garde ideas. Nono's instrumental works, although possessing a certain importance, lack the imaginative, concrete, and personal push, the impulse towards expressive form that one finds in vocal and vocal-dramatic works from *Il Canto sospeso* (1955–1956), a relatively early serial setting of letters by condemned anti-Fascist resistance partisans to the more recent dramatic and semi-dramatic works for voices, instruments, and tape.

The commitment of Maderna and Berio is not only to a view about the social value of art but also to the quality of the new material and the significance of the act of producing it. In addition to being active at Darmstadt, both composers were closely associated with the now moribund electronic studio at the Milan radio station. The electronic experience everywhere profoundly altered attitudes towards serialism and the role of performed music; in Milan, the studio became almost a kind of escape hatch for composers who felt compelled to adopt serial controls but were anxious to find a new, substantial musical matter. Their electronic realizations—those of Maderna and Berio in particular—have the character of improvisations arising out of a direct and fresh experience of the materials. Both composers came back to vocal and instrumental music with something of this attitude, to which was added an intense faith in the expressive and dramatic power of action and gesture as well as the musical form-building potential of word and language. Maderna's opera *Hyperion* (1964), though defective as an over-all conception, illustrates these musical and philosophical tendencies very well: the "protagonist" is a flutist who spends the first ten minutes of the work quietly unpacking piccolo, flute, alto flute, and bass flute; when he finally gets around to the actual act of performance, the sound that gushes forth is in fact an enormously amplified percussive fortissimo (on tape). The piece has a complex choral part—also on tape—with a babbling-of-tongues text made out of isolated words taken from many different languages. There is an instrumental ensemble part and, finally, a long and sensuous—almost Bergian—solo soprano song at the end. In one work for solo flute by

Maderna, the flutist must perform against the pre-recorded image of his own playing. Berio's *Omaggio à Joyce* (1958) is a complex of electronic and vocal sounds pivoted around the sound and shape of the text; *Circles* (1960) is a live setting, for voice and percussionists, of poems by E. E. Cummings in which the physical movements of the performers help to give the piece its performed shape and are conceived for visual and spatial effect; *Passaggio*, his opera for *La Scala*, includes a babble of multi-lingual responses assigned to performers planted in the audience; *Visages* combines on tape electronic sound with a huge range of emotive vocal noise and sound gesture. The tendency of the avant-garde towards theatrical statement and gestural form and the new involvement of musicians in verbal and language problems (sound as language, language as sound, the relationship of meaning to sound and of verbal construction to dramatic-musical form, etc.) are strikingly illustrated by the recent work of these Italian composers; a composer like Berio is everywhere involved with context, significance, dramatic form growing out of meaning.

The long artistic isolation of Eastern European composers is now, it seems safe to say, effectively ended. Avant-garde ideas—although "officially" recognized only in Poland and in the somewhat special case of Yugoslavia[1]—can be found in the music of younger composers in all the Eastern countries including the Soviet Union. The turning point was the bloodless Polish "revolution" of 1956 and the remarkable declaration, by the Polish intelligentsia, of cultural independence from the prevailing policies of artistic and intellectual direction in Eastern Europe. Since that time, Poland has quickly developed what is undoubtedly the most remarkable modern-music life in all of Europe and an important and individual creative production as well. The most striking fact of musical life in Poland today is the amount of contemporary music performed—both in festivals and in normal concert settings—and the size and involvement of its public. Virtually all modern and avant-garde ideas from the West have been well represented in Poland, and Polish composers have available to them an immense variety of resources including a well-equipped electronic studio; well trained, experienced, orchestras; ensembles and soloists with ample rehearsal time at their disposal; and a sympathetic and involved audience. These facts are important in understanding the new Polish music in its variety, its extensive use of resources, and its strong, direct character. Older Polish composers, notably Witold Lutoslawski (b. 1913), Kazimierz Serocki (b. 1922), and Tadeusz Baird (b. 1928), have moved from the development of twelve-tone and serial ideas towards a rich, intense, thoughtful kind of expression, informed by latter-day avant-garde ideas. The younger group—Krzysztof Penderecki (b. 1933), Boguslaw Schäffer (b. 1929), Henryk Gorecki (b. 1933), Wojciech Kilar (b. 1932), and Wlodzimierz Kotonski (b. 1925) (older in fact than Baird but stylistically

---

[1] Although the music of the Yugoslav Milko Kelemen (b. 1924) belongs with that of the Central European composers.

more closely related to the younger generation)—can be characterized by their direct engagement with the *matière sonore*, virtually stripped of everything but its immediate impact as sound. Indeed, the immediacy of this music—undoubtedly a factor in the sure success with the Polish public of a well-managed, effective organization of new ideas—is a source of weakness as well as strength. Thus, the remarkable impression of works like Penderecki's *Threnody for the victims of Hiroshima* (1960) and, to a lesser extent, his String Quartet (1960), with their skillfully managed densities and shifts of string sound and color, must be qualified by the rather more obvious effect of works like his *Stabat Mater* (1962), with its Gregorian motif, spatial choral babbling, and major triad finish, and his Sonata for Cello and Orchestra (1964), with its breathless, herculean slapping, rapping, and tapping, always to great effect to be sure. The work of a composer like Schäffer, involved in a kind of experimental progression of Cageian dimensions—extreme ideas carried to extreme conclusions (a recent piano work lasts eight hours)—seems ultimately concerned with sensuousness of effect rather than profundity of idea. It is probably in the work of the younger composers Gorecki and Kilar, music born of the remarkable richness of the percussive-white-noise Polish language, that the most significant and expressive identity between means and materials can be found.

There are, as yet, no new categories needed for the youngest generation. There are the neo-Realists, the Popsters and the Happeningniks who trade in on the real stuff of the real world to make an existentialist statement: the "Fluxus" group in New York, the younger Italian popsters (notably the Florence group), and several young Germans. There are a number of composers concerned with a kind of Cageian performance-practice music, live-and-tape, conceived in free, spatial terms with performers acting rather than performing on their instruments, every possibility carried to its extreme, mixed, transformed, and even distorted to the limits of perception: the Michigan "Once" group (Gordon Mumma, Robert Ashley, George Cacioppo), a number of New York composers (James Tenney, Malcolm Goldstein), the excellent, somewhat less unified, very individualistic Illinois group (Lejaren Hiller, who works with computers, Johnston, Kenneth Gaburo, Salvatore Martirano), one or two expatriates (notably the pianist-composer Frederic Rzewski), the "underground' Prague group (notably Piotr Kotik), and several young Germans (Dieter Schnebel, Hans Otte, Michael von Biel). There is a kind of "junk music"—an equivalent of junk sculpture—in which the useless and discarded bits and scraps from the junk heap of aural experience are arranged and de-ranged.

There are still the artificers, ever concerned, in a world of shifting values, with the expressive poetry of fantasy, with the act of will in ordering a particular universe of new ideas from the totality of possible perception within the psychological and poetical realities of the act of performance and the experience of sound. It is clear that, in the best work of the younger men and the best recent output of older composers, the newest new music has a new and vital subject matter: the total range of experience. The old categories—serial, aleatory, closed form, open form, chance, and ultra-rationality—are no longer really relevant. For the younger composers, and many of the older ones, the barriers are down, the categories destroyed, the old battles over and done with. Any kind of statement is possible. All possible materials and all possible relationships between creator, creation, performer, and perceiver are possible (including none); but the significance of these possibilities is only to be found in the context of creative definition. In a true sense, the raw material of every new piece is this total possibility of experience; the true subject of the discourse, the quality and nature of experience and perception, and the way we relate and organize these perceptions of experience—i.e. the way we know. The task is not an easy one; but the best music of the twentieth century has always proposed the most difficult, the most profound and universal artistic problems and then resolved them anew. To-day, more than ever, the problems, the materials, the premises and the forms, the expressive means and realizations, the psychological, artistic, esthetic, and human meaning of the new music must be unique to each work of art—established anew with each act of creation and realization and yet universally valid in terms of the scope and universal potential of human experience and knowledge.

Bibliography

For a discussion of some of the "new performed music" in the United States, see the author's report in *Perspectives of New Music* (Spring, 1963); a wider survey of post-war developments in American music, also by the author, appears in *The New American Arts* (New York, 1964). Extensive material on Stockhausen has been published in German, notably the *Texte zur elektronischen und instrumentalen Musik* in the DuMont Dokumente series (Cologne, 1963) and vol. 6 of the Kontrapunkte series (Rodenkirchen, West Germany, 1961). For Boulez, see the composer's own *Penser la musique d'aujourd'hui* (Mainz, 1963). Xenakis has written about his own theories in *Musiques formelles,* but the book is difficult even for able readers of French and is, reportedly, full of mathematical errors. An inquiry into the contemporary situation, including contributions from Old World and New, appeared in the French review *Preuves* over a period of several months from fall to spring, 1965–1966.

Index